Country Living Publications

Portions of this book have been published in Ensign Magazine and broadcast via the nationally syndicated radio segment American Reflections.

To Joel for his patience, perseverance, and publishing moxie: gifts he freely bestowed on 'Swimming the Sun' that it might be a gentle guide of gratitude for all who read it.

Swimming the Sun

A Celebration of Family, a Lake,
and Other Endangered Species

Contents

Prologue:

While making my way to the dock for my morning swim I tried, with little success, to avoid the fresh clods and hillocks of earth left by a recently departed monster-track-hoe. I paused on the steepest part of the downward slope and looked up from the rough earth to inspect the early morning sunrise and the little lake that reflected back every mood and nuance of the world that surrounded it. I greeted the barely ruffled lake. "Good morning, Lake."

I said it quietly while trying to keep my lip movement to a minimum. I smiled because it brought memories of the eleven year old me after I had received my mail order book, Mystify your Friends—Learn the Secret Art of Ventriloquism. Only now I wasn't intent on mystifying anyone, I was just hoping that the neighbors wouldn't see me talking to the lake.

Within a heartbeat I felt a wisp of cool cross my face. I smiled. Greeting acknowledged with affection. Then quickly, but trying to maintain a casual air, I glanced both left and right to see if my neighbors had been watching. As far as I could see they were not. Good. Heaven knows they probably have a too-long list of my idiosyncrasies already filed away. Talking to the lake hopefully won't be added. I have already been teased beyond comfort about doing some Fijian war dance on the end of our dock. It wasn't planned. Sudden discovery of a quorum of quarrelsome earwigs that had taken an overnight lease in my swim trunks precipitated what must have been an eyebrow raising performance. They, my trunks, had spent the night drying on the patio railing—an open invitation for critters that favor dark and dampness. If you've ever looked closely at earwigs they are not particularly pretty, except perhaps to other earwigs. If you've ever viewed them under a magnifying glass, worse yet—you could easily imagine them in some Jurassic setting snapping their prey in half with their lethal rear-end pincers. I now try to remember to give my outside-dried trunks a vigorous shake before I put them on so I will be saved from the graceless exhibit of doing it after.

Yes, my family and I have provided our neighbors with generous amounts of entertainment over the years, virtually all of it spontaneous—occasionally, spontaneous to the point of combustion. By now I was scanning the eastern shore and was thankful that the skyline's silhouette was still graced with some tall and verdant evergreens despite the influx of over one hundred homes since I and my little lake first met. Don't misconstrue the possessive 'my' as legal ownership—heavens no. Struggling to pay taxes, at today's exorbitant rates, for just one lot on the lake is burden enough. No, my 'my' is a sentimentalized and romantic fantasy that exists only in my head and heart, not on the county tax rolls.

What I saw and felt while standing on the brow of the lake convinced me that there were no major threats to the forecaster's promise of "fair and sunny", notwithstanding the low-lying, clumpy fog that was doing its best to collect and rise to some higher status—perhaps cumulous or even cirrus. But even with their best efforts to rise and rain the cloudlets seemed destined to remain loosely-laced and bumbly as the northern breeze chased and scattered them southward.

Almost always a wind or breeze hailing from the north has been the harbinger of fair weather. And so it was today. The low-lying billows commingled easily with the wispy mist that was rising from the lake. The sun, generally, was finding it easy to burnish through the passing vapors. Indeed we might reach the forecasted eighty-five to ninety degrees—hot for the Pacific Northwest but nothing like the triple digits plaguing much of the country. For that I am eternally thankful. Drought, so far this year, has been the least of our worries. But of course in the Pacific Northwest the word drought historically has seldom made an appearance in the lexicons of our web-toed meteorologists. On the fourth of July, just a week ago, it poured buckets—almost a given since our official Northwest summer generally kicks in with some cloud-sparse skies about ten days after the 4th.

When I reached the end of our dock I dropped my towel

onto the wooden planking while I tried to maneuver my feet out of my sandals without bending over. My toes don't seem to take well to their newly assigned tasks, the same tasks that my fingers had happily carried out for the majority of my life. But today, thanks to a back muscle taking offense to the very exercise that was supposed to help prevent such a thing, the ground seemed to be inordinately far away. With the suppleness of youth but a memory, I'm being forced into new niches of creativity while try-ing to do the same things that I've always done, and for the most part, taken for granted. Indeed fond memories of our youth are often viewed through a lens fogged with the hint of remorse.

During my long distance observation of my feet and toes wrestling with Velcro-gripped sandal-straps, I noticed that some of the dock planking had been scorched by heat. The residue of burned black powder covered a good square yard of the dock. I was a bit miffed because I'd asked that the dock be off limits for launching bottle rockets and other pyrotechnics on the fourth, but with excited grandchildren and their equally zealous Dads itching for nightfall and the rockets-red-glare my cautionary request probably didn't even reach a "one" on anyone's scale of priorities.

I realized then, with a mini mental jolt, that it had been a week since the fourth. Where does the time go? I know that phrase is shopworn, but I also know that I'll ask it again and again, beyond counting I suspect. Indeed, where does it go… and go so quickly? I've noted, with a small degree of comfort, it isn't just our contemporary lifestyle that seems to blur the pass-ing of days and years of our life. Over two thousand years ago the ancient American prophet Jacob (7:26) also pondered the fleeting nature of time and life with more than a little sense of awe and bewilderment, " …the time passed away with us, and also our lives passed away like as it were unto us a dream."

Suddenly another visual reminder of another event and an-other time jumped into view. It indeed had a dream-like, almost surreal, quality clinging to it. This visual clue too was on the dock, but closer to the shore. This event marker was only a couple of inches long, a scar about half an inch deep, not very dramatic looking, also created by fire. But this time the scorched plank was not the result of spent fireworks, at least not of the commercial or premeditated kind. This particular burn mark was left by flaming debris that had fallen from the sky. The inferno heat from a fire-engulfed house had propelled this scorching cinder over thirty feet into the air before it lost momentum and landed on our dock. It just so happens that that razed house was ours—a house we had just finished building a mere thirteen months before. The char and ashes were mute but still thunderously stentorian in declaring the brief and fragile nature of earthly stuff.

Suddenly, undoubtedly prompted by memories of our fire-razed home, I turned and looked eastward across the lake and recalled yet another fire. I was thirteen then. The memories and emotions surrounding the events and time began flooding back. I had to squint against the morning sun but still, through a grove of old cedars I could see, a large, relatively new home. It replaced a log cabin—a cabin owned by the Heinz family in the forties and early fifties. It too had burned to the ground. Just south of where the log cabin had once stood the house of my youth still stands. There have been additions and remodeling by subsequent owners but still, compared to some of the behemoths that squat on either side of it even the word modest would cast it in too grand a light. I have no idea what the inside looks like now because I haven't been curious or brave enough to go knock on the door and say, "I wonder if you would mind if I came in and looked around. You see, I grew up in this house."

It seems strange and troubling that even though I lived in that house for eight years I can recall only one specific detail about the interior of the house—it was the oil stove in the hallway between my bedroom and the kitchen. That stove warmed and dried me and my rain-soaked clothes from my tender tenth year until I was eighteen, the year that I graduated from high school and moved to Seattle to go to college. It wasn't just the warmth that I remember about that old stove, there was another literal impression that has stayed with me over the years—it was the pattern left by the stamped metal housing of the stove that scorched my clothes when I got too near or stayed too long. I think that I could still pick out that design because I had more than a few pants and shirts singed with that hot stove brand. My youthful posterior also bore that stove branding more than a few times when on cold winter days I would rush out of the unheated bathroom to stand by the stove to dry off. Amazing how just a fraction of an inch or a nanosecond of time can define the difference between pleasure and pain.

Heinz's fire-ravaged log cabin had stood just twenty yards or so north of my boyhood home, and curiously the Heinz's cabin holds more memories for me than the home of my youth despite the fact that it was only part of my life for a relatively short time. The Heinz's cabin served mostly as a summer retreat for them but occasionally they came in the winter. I always had a sense of heightened anticipation when I saw their car roll down their wooded drive or when I got off the school bus and saw smoke coming out of their chimney. Their living room was filled with books. There were stacks of magazines on the end tables surrounding by the rich patina of well-worn leather furniture. The potpourri of fine furnishing and endless books created its own unique bouquet of fragrances that were intoxicating to my young soul. It seemed that the Heinz's cabin breathed out a rarefied oxygen for all of my senses, I waited for it to exhale so I could take it in. On occasion I was allowed to borrow a National Geographic or Life Magazine from them. It was an exciting and astounding world for me. Mr. Heinz died shortly after we moved in next door so it was Mrs. Heinz and their thirty-something daughter Phyllis that I got to know. In my young memory both women seemed very tall with long faces that seemed to go with their height. They both were kind and I felt that they were very, very sophisticated—a world apart from my family. Not that I had the slightest notion what constituted sophistication or that there was even such a word, but to live in a home surrounded by all of those books and magazines seemed a marvel. The Heinz's bestowed yet another everlasting bit of élan to my life when Phyllis Heinz taught me to swim.

It wasn't long after that that the Heinz's cabin burned to the ground. I wasn't home when it happened, but I was told that when the firefighters arrived they looked through the window and saw the caretaker sitting in a chair with a book in his lap. The flames, by then, had pretty well engulfed the interior of the cabin. It was speculated that he had fallen asleep while smoking. Smoking seemed like such a waste, a life plus hundreds of books gone. One cigarette changed the course of events for not only the caretaker but also for the Heinzes, and perhaps, for me. They didn't rebuild and eventually sold their land. I missed the Heinzes, I missed their books—something positive, something warm, had been taken away.

I was ten when our family of four moved one thousand miles from the foot of the Wasach Range to this small lake north of Seattle. The move was laden with both drama and trauma. My mother provided the trauma by spreading her anti-Northwest misery as easily as I could spread warm blackberry jam on toast. I doubt she ever forgave my father for getting a job in the Everett shipyards, or the Germans and Japanese for starting a war that required ships to be built to stop them.

The drama came when my young senses were bombarded by the everlastingly outrageous Northwest greenery that attacked my vision everywhere I looked. I had left behind winters whose primary colors were white and gray. The valley of my birth waged weather so harsh that even that mighty Muppet, Kermit, couldn't have croaked one chorus of "It's not easy being green" before being flash-frozen to a glacial-gray. Green was only to be heard, never to be seen during the long, winter months.

The other sensory overload that the Pacific Northwest boggled my boyish brain with was water—it was everywhere—from the heavens on down. The only body of water that my pre-teen life knew was the irrigation ditch that flowed to the brimming alongside our front sidewalk once a week in the summer. Still, I never got to know that water very well because of my mother's harsh tales of all the children who had been "drowned in that very ditch…"

My mother's unhappiness with Washington was vented full force against my dad. Perhaps there were other fuels, unknown to me that fired my mother's anger. I didn't know, then nor now. I remember many times, after I had gone to bed, hearing mother's high-pitched assaults. It was the worst sound in the world. I don't remember what was said, but the tone of her voice stabbed through my heart and wrenched at my insides. As the frequency and volume of my mother's woes increased I saw less of my dad. She waged a contest against him to win my affections. I had none of it. I looked more and more toward the lake.

A few years later, my father, forty-nine, died of a stroke. In my youthful angst I blamed my mother. The Lake became my father and my mother. I was nurtured on its shores; its waters were my womb and I was its suckling son. The lake became a passion, a joy, and eventually I felt its sorrow when the influx of people and their things began to destroy the lake's creatures and the habitat that I loved.

Then when I was a senior in high school I did something that I can now look back at and say, "Wow, that was extraordinarily providential." It was a much different story when I was eighteen. Then I said: "Wow, should I really do this? It's going to take every penny I've saved."

Indeed, it was one of those pivotal decisions that at the moment of conception I would have measured in feet, or yards at the most. Now, many years past, no earthly tape measure could encompass what I did as an eighteen year old. The reason is simple, what I did as a high school senior most assuredly determined who my future wife was to be. In fact, the chances that I would have ever met and married Ann Killoran would have been astronomical had I not have scraped together every penny I owned, all four hundred dollars of it, and bought a lot on the west side of the lake half way though my senior year.

There was no road on that side of the lake then, just woods. A little over a decade later Hanley and Geraldine Killoran bought the lot next to mine, the lot that my mother had purchased the same time I bought mine. Their youngest daughter was Ann, the girl I eventually fell in love with and married.

With age and understanding another passion surpassed the lake, not consciously chosen, but certainly childhood-influenced. This passion surpassed the lake in time, energy and thought. The passion is family! Not just my family, but all families—for I weep for the child whose family is not!

In a world so filled with things much bigger than life this book is dedicated to the small—to real life! A manual of downward mobility; a celebration of joy for things and events often unseen and unthought in a world running faster than the speed of light!

Swimming the Sun and Other Small Miracles

The lake, warmer than air, was silently yawning its early morning curls of mist. The far shore was cloaked by the languidly beautiful vapors. My son, rushing to go to work, paused, gazed out on the lake, then said, "The mist on the lake looks really cool."

We watched in companionable silence for a brief moment. I felt his awe and pleasure—a shared flight too soon ended. The ephemeral damplets with their twisting shapes had bare minutes before being warmed to oblivion by the rising orb.

The sun is coming, the sun is coming!

I wanted to be part of the two—to feel as well as see.

Could I be quick enough to join the marriage? Could there be three? Would the lake spit me out for interfering? I rushed to change.

But easing into the water was not a thing to rush. The lake, pristine, untouched by wrinkles, was a sacred thing. I slowly, gently let the water bring me in until it immersed my head. I hated to awaken a lake as breathless as a frightened fawn.

I swam up a conduit of light, eastward, toward the rising, blinding sun. To save my sight I closed my eyes, but before I did I saw whispers of rising mist. I raised my hand to brush them; the damp danced round and through, then gone!

With eyelids squeezed tight, I swam—warmth my guiding star. Then with guarded glances I looked to see how the water caught the sky. Each ripple different, my varying wake continuously changed my image of the sun.

Water lives to move—it moves to live.

My wavelet, always preceding, pushed the reflection of the sun into molten shapes, the outer edges undulating, moving, alive. First, a string of fiery pearls shooting ahead (as though my eyes were cosmic cannons) toward the sun. I tried to count them: seven, eight, nine, twelve.... I stopped so my waves would still; the mirrored sun grew from pearls to apples in size. The quiet space between each ripple enlarged like an opening scroll. The water then gave me back three wavering suns with spider-thin lines of brilliant gold, trailing light shooting from their sides. As I tried to understand the whys of those trailing lights of glory, they were disturbed, then gone.

A breeze had spanked the molten pearls and suns away, but left instead dancing facets, endless to my eye. In an instant, I was floating in a diamond sea. I turned and stroked toward home. I knew I'd swum a treasure. Could I hold it in my mind? Enfold it in my soul? Could I describe it? Would you believe it if I did?

What greater joy could there be
Than to ride the crests of a wind-crossed sea
And talk of life, of love and of you and me

The Christmas Kayak and the N.F.L.

For at least three years running I envisioned decking the bow of my kayak with Christmas lights and touring around the little lake we live on to spread some Christmas spirit.

Well, this year I noticed an ad for strings of battery-powered Christmas lights for $3.50 each. That, I thought, was almost within my budget so I made the trip to town for the lights. The bulbs and strands turned out to be punier in person than depicted in the ad (why wasn't I surprised?) so I had to buy four sets. Then there were the obligatory batteries. Of course, they weren't on sale—again, no surprise. The cost of an illumined Christmas was ascending.

Next, I constructed a small light stand with a center pole to fit the kayak, then I draped the lights from it. I was ready and eager, but the weather didn't cooperate until Monday night. The skies cleared, the mercury dipped, the stars were jewels on velvet. Christmas was in the air!

Loaded with my son's "boom box" and a cassette of carols I headed for the lake with my knit cap pulled over my ears and my down jacket snugged tight. I carefully maneuvered the light-festooned kayak into the cold black waters, then did my balancing act getting in, hoping fervently that I and my electronic entourage wouldn't begin our tour with a baptism.

With "Silent Night" wafting through the December blackness, and bowed by a halo of colored bulbs, I started to paddle slowly around the shore. The first house I approached was virtually all glass in front; surely they would see! But as I neared I saw a vapid flicker of light changing every second or so, dark then bright.

There were five heads silhouetted in front of a giant screen TV. It was Monday night football! My opposition was formidable. But I thought I'd linger a moment, hoping just one of the five might glance outward. I turned up the carol's volume: *"Silent night, holy night, shepherds quake at the sight, glories stream from heaven afar."* The words wafted to their window. I caught my breath and watched.

One face turned toward the Christmas kayak. I could see him, a young boy, gesture toward the lake and tell the others. I waited in anticipation and saw four adult sets of shoulders shrug in indifference. Not one head turned to see the light in the darkness. The faces stayed fixed; probably a spectacular touchdown or a pass held their gaze. Then I looked beyond their blackened silhouettes to see what marvelous thing was gripping their eyes and souls.

Their captor stood boldly bright on the mega-tube, and as the Tabernacle Choir sang *"Silent night, holy night, Son of God, love's pure light, radiant beams from thy holy face...."* I saw beams from their giant screen reflect on their intent faces. It was a commercial that gripped them tight. A commercial for Bud-Lite!

Kayaks and a Family Memory

Our Friday evening with the children had been planned for a week in advance. We had seen ads for a new "G" rated movie that we felt was interesting and appropriate. So it was set. We would see it as a family. When Friday arrived I bought a newspaper to check the theater schedule; to my dismay the movie had been changed! The film we wanted to see had played for barely a week and was gone.

The children were disappointed, and I resolved to find another good movie. After seven phone calls to neighboring towns, resolve turned to dissolve. There was not a film worth seeing within a thirty-mile radius. The children moaned, and I stared out the darkened window.

The night was mellow, but with just enough bite that one could feel the teeth of winter near. And there, shrouded in the October mist, was a beautiful harvest moon. "A perfect night for hide and seek in the kayaks," I suggested.

The children responded enthusiastically, and we got our coats and life jackets and walked down to the old dock. My daughters, six-year-old Alison and three-year-old Leah, slipped into the snug and familiar seats of the double kayak with me. Joel, thirteen, and Jason, eight, took singles.

The moon rose higher above the earth's shadowy horizon, its light made doubly eerie by motionless bands of clouds and the fine wisps of mist that rose from the dark lake. We floated in a dream world, fading in and out of each other's vision. Joel struck out across the lake. The black night and the mist nibbled at him until he was gone. Little Leah shivered against me and snuggled deeper in my lap. I stopped my paddling and shushed Jason and Leah. Our senses strained against the night. The lamps from across the lake gave us shimmers of sight that might show us Joel's stealthy silhouette. We waited and watched.

"There!" Alison shouted as she saw Joel's shadow slip through a line of light. Paddles dipped and splashed. Jason laughed with delight as we raced to head Joel off, but he was gone. The night had defeated us. Excitement sharpened our eyesight; each slight of shadow made us tingle. We paddled hard down the lake, and our breath stayed like balloons behind us to mingle with the mist.

The younger children and I devised some stealth of our own to trap the "rascal" Joel. We paddled as quietly as we could to the shore's edge; there we lurked behind some logs, wishing the moonlight away so Joel would not see us. Between Alison's giggles and Jason's repeated whispers of "where is he, where is he?" we didn't stand a chance. Joel's kayak came cutting through the mist straight toward us. We hooted and cheered as we raced for home.

As we stood once again on the dock and looked over the lovely lake, I pulled my children close and thankfully rated our production "G" for great. That night we were not mere observers before a large screen; we were participants. Our initial disappointment had turned to delight, and our simple fun became a cherished family memory.

The World is So Full of a Number of Things[1]

The winds had cleaned out the sky, and not a feather-wisp of cloud was left to soften the icy glitter of the stars. The mercury shrank small, and deep chills moved through the waters of the lake. By morning the lake was at rest; the waves that had once moved at the back of breezes lay flat, covered with a cold and crystal shell. The turmoil of autumn was stilled, and the peace of winter reflected a steel blue in the crisp of early morning air.

I walked our four-year-old son, Joel, to the edge of the lake. With our heels we scuffed loose pebbles from the frozen sand and laid up a small store of them. Then in the sharp quiet of the frozen morning I shushed him. I cocked my arm and threw. The pebble arched into the silence, hung, then struck. The sound was marvelous. The singing of rock on ice crescendoed across the lake, and the far shore threw it back on an echo. Joel was enthralled, and the enchantment of it captured him as he threw pebble after pebble, their songs racing back to him through the ice and air.

When the pebbles ran out we stopped to look for more. Just then we heard a small stress sound ping through the ice, then the tinkle of ice breaking. As we looked around, we noticed a small furry head pop through the ice under our neighbor's dock. In a moment it was followed by another. The beavers in residence were coming up for a breath of crisp air.

That evening, before the children's bedtime, Ann bundled them up against the night air, and I took them for a walk. An advantage of living in the country is that street lamps don't dim the view of the heavens at night. Besides, that night the moon gave us all the light we need to walk through the woods to the road. Joel clutched my right hand and Amy, his little sister, my left. When we left the cover of trees, Joel looked up and saw the moon.

1 Title taken from the poem "Happy Thoughts" by Robert Louis Stevenson

"Daddy, daddy, somebody took half the moon." He was almost in tears because of the loss. Little Amy took up the chorus in her squeaky little voice and asked, "Why somebody take half moon?"

As I held their warm little hands in mine, we walked down the frosty road and talked. I tried to explain why we could see only half of the moon, and looking down into their upturned faces, I believe they understood. Oh, maybe not about the moon, but they understood that I love them very, very much.

The Miracle of Standing Still
(Hummingbird, a la Calvin)

It was on an early June morning that I stood with garden hose in hand adjusting the spray on some newly-planted mint and thyme. As I was playing the water over the garden I heard an intense whirring sound. I knew the sound well and a smile warmed my face before I even saw my hyper little friend. Within a nanosecond I caught a glimpse of his emerald head, and to my surprise that little hummer of a bird was headed straight for the stream of water coming from the hose. But before he took the full force of the stream he slowed, stopped, and boggled yo-yo-ish up and down, seemingly pondering which trajectory to take through the forceful flow.

He chose the outer, finer, mist—a decision that seemed prudent for such a bantam-weight piece of fluff. His iridescence (dependent on the line of flight and light) was dulled a bit by the mist, and after his run through the sprinkler he stopped, backed slightly, turned, then hovered. Now only a foot or so from my hand, I swear he was considering his next move. I felt his little hummingbird soul decide on a more daring flight—and I was right. This time he went deeper toward the rushing core, and when he emerged his tiny feathers were wet and spiky, and his whirring wings sprayed a mist of their own.

For all the world he reminded me of Calvin (without Hobbes), the irrepressible cartoon character. Now only inches away, he looked me right in the eye and said, "See what a tough guy am I." I actually felt a sting of concern as I anticipated the rashness his hummingbird mind might be hatching. His iridescent reds and greens flashed, then subdued as he maneuvered into place. Now, only a few inches down line from where the solid stream left the brass nozzle, he stared intently at the water, then at me. I felt dare in the air. Then he did what no other bird

of another feather can do. He literally backed up, as though to
get a running start, then with a higher pitched revving he zizzed
straight toward the solid core of the rushing stream.

He hit with a thud. It joggled and tossed him from his
course. A foot or so down stream a tumble-washed hummingbird
emerged as bedraggled as a bit of flotsam. He dazedly sputtered
to a nearby roost to drip dry. I laughed and cheered. That gutsy
little rascal had gone for the gusto. I doubt I'll see him making
any more sprinkler runs soon—unless a sizzling sunny day comes
along and fun looms larger than folly in his little hummingbird
mind. And of course there has to be someone very patiently and
peacefully standing sprinkling their mint and thyme.

Epilogue: July 18th, 1997

Here it is five years after the original close encounter of the
hummingbird kind—ironically only about twenty yards from the
first bird-meets-water episode. It was industrial strength deja-vu; I
was astounded, enchanted, and for a few minutes terrified at what
I was seeing. Once again, (eerily so), I was watering some herbs,
this time on top of the "dome", an earth-berm structure that
houses my office and workshop. Joel, my firstborn, had completed
a patio I started years ago on the berm's roof, and I was damping
down some of the earth. As an almost automatic afterthought I
started watering the half-barrels of rosemary, oregano and lavender that sat at the west end of the patio.

As I was playing a spray of water on the herbs, a streak of
iridescent green came zizzing out of nowhere and hovered a few
feet from the spray of water. My heart leapt! Was I going to see
a replay of my Calvinesque hummingbird? I had just read, two
days prior, my "Miracle of Standing Still" to a church group, and
I couldn't quite believe that I was seeing a replay of that delightful
garden vignette played out just a few yards and a few years from
the original bird-bath incident. This little hummer didn't seem

quite as bold as the previous hummingbird. (Was he the same one? How long do hummingbirds live? So many things to learn!)

This bit of fluff, too, displayed a fascination for a stream of water (perhaps all hummingbirds do), but just a little more reserved. He flew in and out of the of the finer outer mist several times, each time retreating to a distant fir branch before his next sortie. I was beginning to think that this small fellow was a little more prudent than my original bird. He wasn't going to risk all in the main stream of things. Then suddenly he turned and swooped down to the very swath of herbs I was watering only to perch on an oregano stem that was right in the path of the central flow of water. He and the oregano blossoms jittered in the force.

For a brief moment I thought he was enjoying it, then I realized that he was in trouble—deep trouble. In an instant I swerved the hose away and released the valve on the nozzle. He didn't move! Had I killed him? I rushed to the oregano clump and leaned in close to the poor little fellow. He was still upright, clinging tightly to the stem. His eyelids were closed. It struck me how huge his eyes looked in proportion to his soaked head. His feathers were in total disarray, a jumble of sodden, limp little spearlets. In fact, save for his long, gently-curved hummingbird beak, he didn't look like a hummingbird at all. All of his colors were washed out—he was just a lump of damp-down. I leaned closer still. I could actually hear minuscule raspings of air intake. He lived! But his living wasn't easy; he shook and quivered and I wanted to take the poor thing in my hand and dry him off, but thought better of it. I dithered a moment on what to do for my small charge. (I was now feeling fully responsible and fully guilty about my hummer's condition.)

At that moment it dawned that there were two things that I had to do. First, leave him alone; don't touch him! Second, there always seemed to be a doubter whenever I read my "Miracle of Standing Still". I was still feeling the sting of injustice from two days prior when one "Thomas" opined, "Oh, come on, a hummingbird didn't really do all that!"

Evidence. That's what I needed, and it was almost within my grasp. Maybe! I ran down the slope of the dome into the office for my video camera, which I knew had tape and a charged battery in place, ready to go. I puffed back up the hill with camera at the ready. He was still there. I adjusted the camera to digital zoom so I could have a really close look at my super-soaked adventurer. (I don't particularly like the graininess of the digital zoom but it gives you whale-size close-ups) I looked through the lens and could see what appeared to be long, lush eyelashes. "Girls would kill for these," I thought. Then his lids started to quiver, open slightly, then close again. They opened more with each effort. I could feel him trying to assimilate his soggy world, come to grips with unwieldy, waterlogged feathers and a brain battered by hydro-force.

I filmed what seemed like five minutes of his recovery. I noticed a hose coupling behind him which gave a sense of perspective to the tiny wet frailty that filled my viewfinder. A potato bug bugalooed by. I could hear the buzz of a nearby honeybee. I'd slipped into a Lilliputian world. It seemed so peaceful there, so manageable. An illusion I'm sure, but time had slowed to stopping. I hoped my friend would heal quickly—somehow I felt he would. No sooner had I heard this thought than his tiny head began to move slowly back and forth. Until then there had been just a trembling of his frail frame and a blinking of eyes, no head movement at all. I reached my hand down to clear away some foliage and turned to get my camera. There was a rustle, a zizz— he was gone! I saw a ragged and barely recognizable hummingbird head for the fir boughs about sixty feet away.

I was thankful for the warmth of the day and the freshness of the breeze, good things both to dry and heal a bruised and pummeled little hummer. A hummer that had met head-on with a less-than-prudent man who still has much to learn about the small and fragile creatures of this earth.

"Hey, Dude! I Thought You were a Buoy!"

If I could wave my hand and grant myself any wish, the temptation would be to decree "No powerboats on our little lake—ever!" That would certainly bring more peace and serenity to the lake, less frustration and turmoil, and perhaps the western box turtle and the otters might return. Perhaps. But would it make me any happier? I suspect that it would, but of course I can't be certain. One thing for sure, the excitement factor would certainly subside.

I don't begrudge others having fun, but I do take umbrage when their fun becomes tantamount to terrorization. For example, not long after our neighbors had a new dock constructed a beautiful day dawned, the temperature climbed to the eighties, and with the climbing temperature so did my desire to go swimming. I checked the lake for boat activity: minimal. I went in to change into my suit. As I walked into the lake I noticed our neighbor's son and some of his friends had encamped on their dock. Not a problem.

They were also drinking beer. Hmmm, maybe a problem, for they had also hauled a jet ski into the lake. Obviously jet skis were not meant to be just decorative. (I hasten to insert that I have wonderful neighbors—I couldn't imagine any better. It's their son's friends that come into question.) I felt a sense of unease as I started swimming down the lake, but the cool water and glow of the sun commingled to massage my mind and body. My salubrious swim was overcoming the dull nag to the point that I actually smiled and waved at the boys on the dock as I swam by. They waved back, lifted their beer cans and fired up the jet-ski, in that order. The nag returned.

As I swam away from the dock the high whine of the jet ski cursed the air. I noticed, lamentably, that they seemed to be doing

what jet skiers do best around the docks. No "beyond the safety
of the buoy markers" for those booze-emboldened water warriors.
The lake near them was afroth with dizzying speed, tight turns
and sluing into hairbreadth misses. I was thankful for each stroke
that took me away from the maelstrom. I dreaded the return
home. By the time I had reached the Massart's cove on the south-
west corner of the lake I noticed the jet-skiers had broadened
their arc of activity.

My chance of sneaking through the buzz cutters had broadened, I thought. Halfway home I was astounded to see the jet-ski,
full-throttle, homing in on me! I was well within the buoy boundaries, why weren't they well within the boundaries on the other
side!? Could it be the beer and stupidity or is it stupidity plus the
beer? At that moment it didn't make any difference. I was scared
spitless! I stopped swimming. I kicked as hard as I could to push
my torso out of the water and started waving my arms and yell-
ing.

Still he bore down on me like some crazed hornet! I could
see his face and his longish blond hair clearly, as though a powerful zoom lens had suddenly focused. He was even close enough
for me to see some pimples on his forehead. (Were they pustules
of some malignant growth oozing from his brain?) Then I noticed
some recognition, or a dawning on his face and with a jerk (a
reference to the movement not the person) the power ski slued to
one side. The spray hit my face and the rogue wave slammed over
me. The jet-ski did not—amazing! I am finding, as of late, that
swimming Shoecraft is affording me many and repeated opportu-
nities to feel great outpourings of relief and thanksgiving—more
than I really care to have.

And what of my would-be slay-rider? He gave a quick fur-
tive glance back at me, then cranked up the volume and speed
and continued on his mindless way. I wondered if in his numbed
mind he could even imagine an impaled swimmer on the bow of
his Kawasaki?

Do people who maim or almost maim have no sense of apology, no feeling of remorse for what did or could have happened? The hit and run syndrome was alive and well on the shores of Shoecraft.

By the time I had swum back to the neighbors dock my "Atilla the Hydro-Hun" was reclining on the dock drinking yet another beer. (What else?) Fortunately on the way back to that point the lake some thoughtful prayer had worked a minor miracle on my mind and attitude. My anger, amazingly, was at low ebb. I inquired as dispassionately as possible, as I treaded the very water that he had despoiled just moments before, "You came pretty close to hitting me out there. Why?"

"Hey, dude," he slurred, "I thought you were a buoy. I was just going to jump you."

"Since when do buoys have hair and arms?" I asked acidly. (I instantly considered that hair may have been a moot point, since my pate wasn't exactly plentiful with the stuff, but arms, surely he could see arms?)

He burbled back, "Well, you sure looked like a buoy ta' me."

It was obvious that the lad was looking through ale-colored glasses. I told him with some heat that he was breaking the law mightily by drinking and operating a power craft.

As I spoke he slowly slid his beer can behind his back as if its lack of presence would somehow make me and the problems go away. It didn't. I carefully explained the lake rules for operating jet skis. I also told him that I was contemplating calling the sheriff. He squirmed. I enjoyed his squirm.

As I left the neighbor's dock area and swam toward our beach I glanced back just as he was surreptitiously trying to slip his beer can into the lake without me seeing or hearing. Poor little lake: used, then abused.

There must be a special place reserved after this life for the likes of my earth-trashing yahoo. If I could have a say in its design I'd recommend a very small planet with no fresh water—just stagnant ponds fetid with stale beer and abrim with noxious insects and empty beer cans.

Should the troubled souls who perceive the error of their ways and become determined to pursue a gentler, more considerate and responsible way of life be allowed to leave this hellish place? I think I'll let the serene and gentle spirits of pristine lakes lost and maimed by egregious man hold court over that decision.

However they rule, I'll find it refreshing.

The Supersonic Slug

Morning view
Silvered labyrinth of trails
Mark the paths of gooey snails...
Green-grass gorged and fatted some
On rows of dainty chrysanthemum

As I write, screams are puncturing the walls of my stone-walled, well-insulated office. Leah and Sarah Daniels, her friend staying over the weekend, started a Saturday afternoon game of badminton. Somehow Sarah got the "slick" notion of using the badminton racket to scoop a slug, of which there are multitudes, off the rain-damped lawn. (It had poured all night and this morning.) As the almost supersonic slug (this in no way alludes to the Seattle NBA team) slippery-soared toward my fourteen year old daughter, she decided to seize the slimy moment, so to speak. She smashed the slug back to Sarah. The wad of smooch sailed over Sarah's head into our neighbor's immaculate and pest-free yard—a blight on perfection.

Their gales of hysterical laughter prompted an impromptu retreat to the bathroom by Sarah. Upon her return they started a wild slug-fest the likes of which the world has never seen and hopefully will never see again. The more dissected or decimated the slug, the higher pitched the squeals of laughter. They determined the winner of the slugminton match by examining the strings of their rackets. The one with strings most glopped with gore was the obvious winner. I insisted they hose and disinfect the rackets. The lawn is a gruesome graveyard of gore which only months of sizzling sun will dehydrate and heal.

I asked Sarah and Leah if they had learned anything from the whole mess?

"Yes," they smiled sweetly. "It takes at least two good whacks with the racket before a slug starts losing its guts, and the smaller the slug the better its staying power." Hmm, priceless wisdom for the ages.

What did I learn? The delicate nature of women is as elusive as a slug in compost—especially when they're having fun.

Hearing through your Nose, and other Every-Day Phenomena

I rushed to get into the lake before the killer boats started shredding the surface and churning and chopping all the creatures beneath. The lake was sleeping-dove calm when I started my swim; by the time I had reached the curve of Ellis' point a playful breeze began spanking the surface around me. I rolled to my back to feel the sun on my face and let my head relax into the watery pillow. A small oval window of air rested across my nose and lips-my connection with breath and life.

I continued to swim with a slim slice of face above the water, ears and all else below. I exulted in the flow of water across my back. Suddenly a stiffer breeze hit the water and I heard its roar and whistle loud and clear. Then the thought: how could I hear such a blast of wind with my ears under water? Water carries sound, I reasoned.

Yes, that must be it. But a whistle like wind through a cracked door, like a breathy flute? Hmmm, could it really be? Then I heard it again. The noise rattled loud in my head, but it wasn't always there. Even when I felt the breeze cross my face and saw the wrinkled water, I didn't always hear the wind-some roar. Were my water-logged senses deceiving me? Why the intermittent sound?

Again I felt the gust and heard the noise. I shifted my head so the wind was hitting the side of my face. The rushing stopped. The roar? No more! Ta-da, problem solved! The answer seemed silly; who would believe? I was hearing through my nose! I tested and retested. I experimented: If I did the backstroke, going with the breeze, my nose, like some fleshy flute-snoot (or would it be a snoot-flute) picked up the scampy breeze and let it whistle in my head. If I plugged my nose or turned my head away from the breeze the song would stop. I was charmed by the concept.

Saner souls would probably be repulsed by the concept of listening through an appendage meant for smelling and blowing. Ah, but not me.

The wind abated. The song died. I was delighted by my new knowledge, but knew my sanity would be questioned if I revealed it to a soul.

On the swim home from the end of the lake I started experimenting with other water and air sounds. I clapped broad handfuls of air into the water and forced it down as deep as my arms could push. My submerged ears could hear the beginnings of tinkling. Bassy to begin with, the pitch rose as the bubbles neared the surface. Was it the Doppler Effect that made the pitch rise? Was it the bubbles growing larger as they neared the surface?

When my bubbles of sound reached the surface the music stopped. Their watery prison burst wide, the sound evaporated into the air and endless space. Between the fluid tones of rising bubbles I turned my nostrils to the wind. No, it wasn't Bach nor Beethoven, not the Beatles nor Benny Goodman, just a simple symphony of sound while swimming Shoecraft—and the sun!

Running Faster than the Speed of Light

Just a moment after I had abandoned my apple tree debudding, (one of my never-ending but seemingly effete efforts to get my apple trees to live up to their name.) I heard the soft lapping of waves against something moving against the wind. If that sounds like a pretty piece of fiction, it is not.

Ask anyone who lives on the shores of a lake who has the soul of an observer, and they will tell you that you can discern the sounds of a craft, even small and stealthy ones, coming into the wind. The waves, large or small, lap with noisy tongues against the moving hulls and set up a watery chorus that can't or won't be muted unless the craft relents and goes the way of the wind and water. I realized that I was hearing a whispery little chorus, pianissimo, but definitely there.

The shore of the lake was hidden from my view by some ever-encroaching salmon-berry vines, but I could hear the faint buffetings of water pushed by a gentle breeze against something small, but moving toward me.

Then I heard short bursts of higher pitched notes—a cacophony of them. A smile quickly surfaced, and I'm sure I grinned broadly in anticipation of what I knew would swarm into view if I but waited a moment or two. They came: two, four, seven, ten baby mallards all yellow and black fuzz scurrying and putting through the water like tightly-wound toys.

They all, to a duck, had small horizontal grayish-black racing stripes starting before their eyes and sweeping an inch or so beyond. I imagined God laughing as he added that sporting touch to lend some dash and visual flair. I smile automatically every time I see them, racing stripe and all, skimming across the lake's fluid shell.

There is so much humor and joy even in the smallest things,

but they are seen and heard so seldom and by so few. How have we let ourselves become so obsessed with running—running faster than the speed of light?

The Case of the Killer Party Balloons

I was miffed that my daughter's school chose to have a full-blown graduation exercise for eighth graders. Soon children will have all of life's experiences thrust on them before they are ten. The world is now burgeoning with eleven year olds who can honestly say, "been there, done that," to virtually any situation of which you might dream. Childhood is so brief, why do adults forever foist fore-shortenings on those tender years?

Well, despite my grousing I had an eighth grade graduation to attend in the middle of my workday. Ann suggested a balloon bouquet for the graduate. I said, "Sure, I'll pick them up." I quickly discovered that virtually every store in the mall has a helium tank eager to blow up balloons—and their prices—in equal proportions. With double inflation I marveled that the mall wasn't torn from its foundation and propelled into outer space.

Then there was the wait to inflate that I didn't anticipate. Running very late, I jogged to the car with my balloon entourage all aflutter. I stuffed them in front of me, put the pedal to the metal, and headed up the road. It was muggy in the car so I rolled down the window. Big mistake! Suddenly the balloons (air-heads all) had a mind of their own. One swiftly moved between my head and the windshield. I was blinded. I tried to grab at the strings, but the sight-robbing balloon was instantly sucked out of the window. That balloon being connected to the rest of the bunch, instantly two more of the air-heads were jerked in front of me. The tether from the escapee was wrapped around my neck, choking me while I was frantically trying to swipe away the inane smiley-face balloon blocking my vision. I tromped on the brakes to avoid passing out or crashing into someone.

Praise be to heaven, no one was behind me. I pulled in the shiny Mylar balloons and once again the yellow smiley-faced one popped up between me and the windshield. It was instant affirmation that those shiny floaty baubles were indeed heliums from hell.

The Everlasting and Agonizing Saga of Bad Bucky and His Buddies!

I suspect it's all part of a giant pay-back scheme that some of the hosts of heaven concocted just for me. The reason? Retribution! Yes, retribution pure and simple—and all because of a very small giggle. Well, perhaps neither "small" nor "giggle" is totally accurate, but my glee certainly wasn't premeditated or cloaked in malice. In short, I've become the victim of my own tweaked sense of humor.

The scary part of all this is that the duration and weight of my reparation seems to lie solely in the hands (paws?) of a band of voracious, single-minded, fur-brained critters.

In retrospect, I'm now convinced that all of nature may have joined forces to bring me low. I even suspect that the leafless alders and the frost-nibbled blackberry vines patrolling the borders of our road that chill December, probably perceived my mirth more as an unrestrained guffaw—a real rankle to them while mourning the loss of a kindred spirit. You see, I was still smiling half a mile later as I opened the door to the warm comfort of our home. I fairly bubbled (to me the telling is more fun than the reality) as I regaled my family with my tale of our neighbor's missing apple tree.

He, my neighbor, was madder than hops. In fact, he did an angry stomp around the pile of chips that were scattered about the well-gnawed stump—about as close to a hop as you can get without actually doing it. I suspect the apple tree wasn't all that pleased either, having been cut off from both its sap and its genealogy on a rather permanent basis.

I guess what tickled me most about the AWOL apple was the fact that the tree was probably some three hundred feet from the lake, and an eager beaver or two had trundled that far inland to find an innocent Gravenstein serenely enjoying its winter respite. I tried to imagine the tree's surprise, having thought that it had given its all for the fall harvest, suddenly finding bad Bucky and his buddies demanding the ultimate sacrifice.

The retelling of my neighbor's woe got better each time until—until that fateful day when the beaver tail (or tale) turned.

I was standing on our front deck looking out over the lake and I suddenly noticed that our view had expanded. Our front yard seemed to have that clean-shaven look. It took me a few minutes to figure it out. Bucky and his buddies had mustered forces and wreaked their distinctive brand of destruction. Surely my unrestrained glee at my neighbor's loss had filtered through to the courts on high. My pay-back had begun. The pair of filbert trees (the proper pairing is important to filberts, I'm told) that I had planted three years prior were gone! Zero, zilch, nothing, and nary a nut had been born to either one of them.

I ran to the front yard with panic rising. My babies were gone! I had watered, tended, fertilized, even encouraged nut-like courtship and now there was nothing. Not one leaf remained. But Miss Manners would have been pleased. The beavers had been meticulous while snacking on my tender filberts. Not a morsel cluttered the ground. I looked at my gizmo-laden watch and the chronographic calendar clearly assessed that it had taken only three weeks for the irrevocable laws of retribution to come my way.

Was I humbled? Was the dawning of sympathy and understanding for my neighbor beginning? Had I learned my lesson? Evidently not! The next onslaught came by air.

Robber Barons from the Sky

They came on August 23rd this year, five years since the frontal foray of our front yard by Bucky and his gang. Last year they came on the 27th—the summer hadn't been quite as sunny and dry. In fact, if I flip through my old office calendars I can tell you the exact day of their obnoxious coming for the last five years. I've circled those days in black- solid black. They are raucous, rapacious, rotten robber-jays.

They always know the very day, perhaps the very moment that my nubile filberts have filled out to perfection and are ready for the plucking. Darn their feathered hides! It was tough enough when I had to suffer and fret my filberts' tenuous beginnings.

However, all was not lost! The beavers had won the battle but not the war. My filberts had roots. Boy, did they have roots. (Alex Haley and the Mormons would have been exhilarated.) By next spring a dozen new shoots were soaring skyward. I fenced and wired to discourage any eager beavers—and waited!

I waited five more years and prayed that the trees would remember their gender and that the catkins would do their pollinating best. Finally they did. I rejoiced. I told my family we were going to have nuts for Thanksgiving. I told my neighbors I would share.

Nuts! From that moment on, my tree and me (bad grammar, but nice sound) were marked men—so to speak.

Every morning I hear the jays doing their orgulous strut up and down the branches, and what prickles me most is the raucous screech that precedes the plucking of each nut. A fairly apt description of that chilling sound is something akin to a monster scratching his brittle fingernails across a roughened, hollow blackboard. It's terrible. Then, of course, the jays fly into the protective bower of our neighbor's cedar branches to eat their hot nuts. There is no question that jays are an endangered species—at least the jays that show up at my house are. I've considered sling shots, air pistols and BB guns, but since I'm not big on guns I just haven't brought myself to give it a shot. But at the end of this last season of devastation I was more sorely tempted than ever before. But then the jays invited friends! Four jays waged a continuous airlift. My poor trees looked like O'Hare at peak time.

Well, I didn't succumb to blasting those blooming blue hellions out of the sky, but I certainly wouldn't mind making a sweet offer to anyone so inclined. Consider this, you hunters: approximately two-hundred pounds of filberts grace my trees every fall. Divide that between the four jays that showed up this year. Intriguing huh?

So be you a hunter or just enhungered, or both, if you see a fifty-pound jay fly over, imagine the succulent nut-stuffed bird on your Thanksgiving table wafting the autumnal aroma of filberts through your house. Go ahead. Give it a shot. Be my guest.

Boredom, Beer and Seeing the Beauty Within

Our local daily newspaper, to which I don't subscribe (I get them from my neighbor to use as packing for a lovely old hand grain mill that I manufacture) ran a two-page spread on high school seniors and their party habits. It low-lighted teens (the article hinted that it was the majority of seniors) who seemingly felt beholden to several breweries, which spend *millions* (usually during sports events), on salacious come-ons with the hopes of hooking the young and holding the old. The breweries are grandly successful in teaching our nation how to fail.

"Parties are where it's at," they say. Mindless, numbing, ultimately esteem-destroying, boozy parties are constantly touted as the epitome for successful living by the brew-mongers.

The most quoted rationale for teens' weekly numbing? "We're bored!"

Do I have compassion for those who are bored and drowning in ennui? Some, if they are young, because they probably learned it from adults—if not the ones they live with then surely from the adults being portrayed on screens big and small. Being bored is a self-imposed mental drought, a mind willfully unwatered by imagination or ambition. A shrinking brain! What an ugly wither.

The Hopis once embraced a lovely way of seeing beyond worldly boredom. Hopefully the Hopi youth are still being taught to embrace and practice it:

"Memorize the Earth. Settle your eyes on a place and learn it. See it under the snow, and when first grass is growing, and as the rain falls on it. Feel it and smell it, walk on it, touch the stones, and it will be with you forever. When you are far away, you can call it back. When you need it, it is there in your mind. Touch it with your mind. Inhale the air that moves across it. Listen to the sounds it makes.

This hogan* will be a blessed hogan
It will become a hogan of dawn
Dawn boy will live in beauty in it
It will be a hogan of white corn
It will be a hogan of soft goods
It will be a hogan of crystal water
It will be a hogan of long-life and happiness
It will be a hogan with beauty above it
It will be a hogan with beauty all around

As I was reading the Hopi blessing, I realized it had a powerful familiarity. In fact I was trying to marry it to a tune I knew well. No wonder, the text of the music running through my head was strikingly similar to the Hopi text, one I had sung hundreds of times. Here's the second verse of this lovely old hymn written by John Hugh McNaughton in the late eighteen-hundreds.

In the cottage there is joy when there's love at home
Hate and envy ne'er annoy when there's love at home
Roses bloom beneath our feet
All the earth's a garden sweet

Making life a bliss complete, when there's love at home
Love at home, love at home
Making life a bliss complete when there's love at home**

What human who has listened or felt but briefly to the spirit of sense and serenity wouldn't long for the abodes hoped for by the Hopis or the Mormons? Why are we so easily swayed by the commercialism whose every breath says *things* are happiness?

---

* An Indian lodge
** Hymns of the Church of Jesus Christ of Latter Day Saints pp. 294

Tales from the Orchardist

An orchardist told me that fruit trees will bear more consistently and vigorously year after year if you thin out the buds to about one apple every four or five inches. With that concept in mind I headed toward the three apple trees growing near the shore of the lake. I twisted and pinched and let fall to the earth the tiny, nubile, green apples-in-the-making that were crowding the more solid, larger applets. As I snipped and twisted, watching all those never-to-be-apples falling fatally to the ground gave rise to a worrisome vision, a vision that seemed bathed from behind with a sickly green light.

Does the orchardist really know what he's talking about? Am I decimating my fruit crop for some pie-in-the-sky (preferably apple) theory? After all, what if a late frost nips everything in the bud? Not withstanding all my thinning and budding I would get zero, nada, zip, zilch, nothing when the fall harvest comes. And insects! Yes, an army of tent caterpillars could munch away every vestige of green despite my prudish pruning.

As I stared at all the disregarded little-green soldiers of misfortune lying on the ground, a vision of our pantry shelves bereft of golden applesauce superimposed itself over them. I jerked my eyes away, but my mind lingered: chicken baked on a bed of sour-creamed mushrooms and rice without a side dish of creamy apple sauce was a barren thought. For Jaime and Jason, the very idea of apple sauceless meals would be akin to child abuse.

I couldn't go on. Sauceless Sunday dinners were too horrible to think about. I couldn't take any chances; I started leaving more applets on the tree. After all, if Mother Nature wants to give a bounteous crop this year I'd better take it and put it by to prepare for the coming apple famine. At that moment I saw two fuzzy, yellowish caterpillars with black ribbing beneath, both inching their way toward the Jonagold tree I was laboring over. That did it! I wasn't going to mess with nature! It was obviously a sign of the upcoming caterpillar onslaught. We were going to need every last apple I could glean. I abandoned the thinning process with a sense of relief. Besides, do you realize how much work it is and how long it takes to thin just one apple tree?

Epilogue: *We had a bumper crop of good-sized apples that year. The next year was a beautiful year with nary a caterpillar's tent in sight, but the apples were few and puny. Hmm! It has been said that, "Man is the only animal that can learn from others' mistakes, but doesn't!"*

When Butterflies Fly Through Rainbows They Speak So You Can Hear

I was carefully sprinkling a newly-seeded patch of garden when my eye was caught by the beautiful black and yellow wings of a butterfly flitting by. The tiger stripes, and the teardrop ends of the trailing tail were there. A Western Tiger Swallowtail, I thought. Fervently I willed the butterfly to stay, and as on command, it turned and gave an extra beat, coming toward the sprinkler in my hand. It flew right through the fine mist playing from the nozzle, and I prayed its parchment wings wouldn't damp beyond repair. To my relief it lightly winged its way to a nearby patch of peppermint and supped on its nectar.

Then, to my amazement, back it came to the outer areola of nozzle mist. As the butterfly hovered there, the watery prisms caught the sun and bowed the colors to my eye. And at that moment, as the Swallowtail with its blacks and yellows fluttered through that fine rain again, I heard laughter of delight. I looked beyond, and there my Jaime, only eight, was running through the sprinkler on the lawn. The Swallowtail lingered and I felt it say, "Ten, only ten, is the total of my days." And beyond the butterfly and rainbow I could see that in the reckoning of eternity, a child's flight by our side is just as brief. We must take, no *make,* the time to watch, else we miss the moments when our child takes flight within the bows of heavenly color and its trailing light.

Setting the stage of your mind: *Several months prior to the 'butterfly-rainbow' incident, Rodale press sent me a promotional copy of a richly illustrated book on butterflies by Marcus Scheck. I was fascinated and charmed by the color plates and the butterfly lore. Example: butterflies (that's the adult stage) live an average of only two to three weeks, some varieties only ten days.*

I suspect the preceding story would never have been perceived, let alone written, if my mental stage had not been arranged and lighted by Scheck's book. So it must be with all that
we do or say. If we have allowed the stage of our mind to be well
illumined and filled with a set and scenery that evokes good,
beauty and knowledge, then it begs to be built upon. Then at a
moment's notice you would be willing to draw the curtains of
your thoughts wide for all the world to see and know. Scary? Of
course, but particularly scary if we allow our mind to be decorat-
ed with the dark, the tawdry, the obscene, the selfish, the violent.
Then our mind's veil becomes leaden and the last thing that
we would ever want is to have those darkish thoughts revealed,
particularly to those who are virtuous—to the children, to those
filled with light.

Toys Are Us

It was an afternoon graced with an unfettered August sun and a northern breeze, a breeze just strong enough to keep elevating an endless phalanx of watery wrinkles. The 'out of the north' breeze brought whispered promises of continued cloudless skies. My daughter Amy, about three, and her older brother were playing in the lake; both were standing in water up to their knees on our gently sloping shore. I was a few yards away, trunks on, pulling some weeds, but ready to do some serious swimming after the children had gotten their fill of splashing.

Over the squeals of the kids I heard the roar of an outboard and looked up and saw a big, deep-hulled ski boat going by about two hundred feet from the shore.

Every time I saw or heard another speedboat on the lake a shadow seemed to pass over my soul. I knew that there was an eight-mile-an-hour speed limit on our small lake; this craft was going closer to thirty[2]. I was angry because speed limit signs were posted on the lake near the public entrance and more and more people were bringing large craft onto the water anyhow. It passed, and my eyes and hands moved back to an onerous salmonberry root that was proving to be much longer and tougher than my patience.

I suddenly heard a short Amy-scream, then abrupt silence. I looked and leapt into the lake in the same moment. A large wake-caused wave had washed ashore and literally toppled little Amy over into the water. If I hadn't been standing close by she could easily have drowned. I was too busy ministering to little Amy to find out who owned the boat.

Does mere ownership of a mega-powered craft give license to unrelentingly plow the shallow, small lakes? Certainly there

2 *When I was young there were signs posting the eight mile an hour speed limit.*

are more than enough bodies of water in the Pacific Northwest that can afford water skiers ample room to maneuver, but still give space and grace for the lesser creatures that long for joy and sustenance within the protective womb of the lake.

Close Encounters of the Worst Kind

I had started for my morning swim about ten after eight—later than I wanted, but I thought I could still get back in time to beat the dreaded 9 a.m. start time for the water skiers. I decided to swim to the north end of the lake this time because there was a breeze coming from that direction and I liked to be homeward bound with the help of the wind and waves.

The weather was perfect. The water was 76 degrees, (almost too warm for me) and just a few, small, insignificantly thin clouds had dared float out into the forever blue. I decided to do a back stroke so I could watch and marvel. I rolled over, eyes to the sky.

I was less than a hundred feet from the lakeward end of the docks, which sprouted out from the shore, and several hundred feet from the buoy-line—that magic line that all speedboats and jet skis were supposed to stay on the other side of as they engage in their power play.

In my mind everything was with me; I was well within my comfort and safety zone. After all, I had almost an hour of boat-ban time, and even if that was ignored, which it often was, I was still within the no-boat zone. I swam and enjoyed, but soon I began to be irritated by my seeming inability to keep in a straight line. I kept veering in toward the docks. Since my right side is naturally stronger than my left this didn't make sense to me. Swimming on my back, I normally compensate by easing off slightly with my right arm to maintain a relatively even course. It just wasn't working. The harder I tried to hold a straight trajectory down the lake the more difficult it seemed. I started getting angry with myself. I virtually let my left arm go limp while I concentrated on getting the maximum strength into my right side so I could stay away from the docks. My efforts were vain—it was as though some tidal force was irrevocably shoving shoreward. It was

at that moment that the lake transmitted to my submerged ears
the pulsing, hydro-pounding vibrations of a speed boat. The noise
was loud, very close.

I immediately rolled and saw the large bow of a deep-hulled
Bayliner headed right toward me. The speed boat had been
gunned, pedal to the metal, to maximum power in order to pull
a skier to the surface. There were five people in the boat—all
looking back to see if the young skier was going to stay up. I was
gripped by sheer terror as I saw and felt two-hundred horses of
piston-power lunge toward me. I had less than a second before the
ton of fiberglass and humanity would be on top of me. I heaved
and willed my body shoreward, and somewhere from within my
soul a piercing sound escaped. I knew intuitively that no one in
the roaring speed boat could possibly hear me, but scream I did as
the gleaming hull took on the form of some hell-begotten guillo-
tine slicing through the water—and me!

Then with thoughts of family, love, God, and so much left
undone flooding through my mind, the killer craft suddenly
veered out toward the buoy-line and center of the lake. The heavy

wake washed over me and for a moment I was totally submerged. As my head popped out of the foam the stern of the boat was just churning by, and I looked up to see a young girl catch sight of me. One of her hands flew to her mouth and the other pointed to me. Two others glanced in my direction but the craft sped on. No, "Are you okay?" "We're sorry, We didn't see you." They were too busy cheering the noble lad who had managed to stay on his skis despite the thoughtless clutter swimming the lake.

Relief thrilled through me —I was safe! Whole! I had both arms and legs! I wasn't gutted out like a fresh-caught salmon! Then the anger started to rise like bile. Year after year I had pled at our lake's recreational rules committee meeting to have skiers start and finish their ski run inside the circle of marker buoys. That way swimmers and people in small boats could have a somewhat safe haven to enjoy the lake. Every year there were supercilious hues of outrage that such an inconvenience would be laid upon the folk with mega-buck ski boats. No one managed to perceive the inconvenience of living without the use of an arm or leg—or the ultimate inconvenience of no life at all!

My whole body felt leaden; I was struggling to stay afloat. I realized that my dark thoughts were pulling me down. I was threatened with drowning again, but this time in my own miasma. I tried to shake my heavy thoughts loose so I could enjoy my swim home, so I could reflect on my blessings. As I looked homeward I saw the retreating boat.

Suddenly I realized that the lake was now windless and its still surface (save for the wake of the ski-boat that was now pounding the shore) preserved in place the bubbled path where the slicing prop had passed. The line of foam corresponded exactly with the path that I would have swum had not some unseen hand forced me shoreward. I thanked God that he had seen fit to preserve my limbs and perhaps my life. I thank him still, every time I think of the day he nudged (pushed might be more accurate) me from my own ill-determined course into a longer and hopefully more productive path!

The Creatures of Shoecraft

It is written that the meek shall inherit the earth. I like that idea. I also passionately want to believe that it is true. My biggest problem may be fitting all of the various pieces of myself into the mold of the meek. If perchance that ever happens (and it may take the miracle of death and the trials that oft proceed it for me to truly master meekness), I look forward to coming back often to visit my little lake. Why would I want to visit a spot jammed with things and the despoilization that things seem to bring? Why, indeed?

Because I have the abiding faith that the day will surely come that the lake and others like it will be restored and refreshed to their original pristine goodness. Perhaps it will require a millennial healing; perhaps the black goo that drives the pulse of the world will be dammed forever when the ever-threatening Mid-East cauldron explodes and topples the very foundations of commerce. Perhaps, perhaps. There are a lot of perhapses and one or more of them could easily incubate the seeds of restoration and refreshing. The day of refreshing and restoration will surely come, I know, for betimes even the lowliest of we humans are afforded glimpses beyond the amnesia of our mortality.

Yes, I would like the opportunity to return and observe, see the beauty when I may commune with the creatures that have been innately equipped to eke out a niche of existence amidst the clutter, and visit with those who will eventually find their way home.

It's not all futuristic, there is still beauty *here and now.* Despite the onslaughts of man, the springs carrying water from the graveled bowels of the Cascade Range keep the lake amazingly clean and marvelously swimmable. Still there are the verdant evergreens, still the rain falls to wash the earth, still there is peace amidst the clutter of sound and senselessness.

But today is today, and those with vision only the breadth of a dollar bill will continue to tow in *lake-and-people killers* in the wake of their affluence. Does affluence have to equal effluvium? For now, it seems it does. But just for now.

The list of the missing in action is long: The wonderfully playful otters, giant catfish, the wily and tough cutthroat, cougars, red fox, deer (there are still a few around), bear, and an occasional swan would grace the lake with its beauty. Ah, and how could I forget the Western Painted box turtle. I once knew every log that they sunned themselves on. Their undersides were an intense reddish pattern that always fascinated me. The wake of large-hulled boats has systematically wiped out the shores where the turtle eggs are nested. The wake has become a wake.

The small four-room house of my youth, too, is a survivor. It was about seventy feet from the shore of the lake. The lake was the magnet that seemed to pull both the creatures and me. In my young mind, the wildest and most elusive of them all was the cougar. In mother's mind, I'm sure there were times that she thought that I was the wildest and most unfathomable of all the creatures of Shoecraft. The thought didn't displease me.

There were times that I believed that the cougar's "wildness" was more my imagination than fact. But then came the heart-pounding news of a nine-year-old girl being mauled to death by a cougar on Camano Island—a mere eighteen miles from our home. She was just a year younger than I.

My imagination went into overdrive with the grisly image of the cougar attacking a pretty blonde girl. Often in my mind the blonde girl turned out to be me. Her picture, showing her in a white ruffly dress, was in the newspaper. From that time, whenever I ventured outdoors at night, my common ol' scared-at-night goose-bumps gave way to a much larger and quiveringly robust cougar-bumps. Never mind that the girl was attacked at high noon on a sunny day, nighttime's shadows hid the most horrible and gruesome monsters that my ten-year-old soul could conjure up.

Walking to or from my Uncle Paul's place after dark had always been a little spooky—suddenly it became downright exhilarating in a very scary way. Uncle Paul and Aunt Florence (my mother's sister) lived about half a mile south of our place on a little cove that had its western shore formed by a small island owned by the Schulenbergs. In the summertime when the water level of the lake was low I could walk along the shoreline to and from home. In winter the road was the only way home unless I wanted to row the boat.

Since there were only about a dozen houses on the lake, that meant that few cars pierced the night with their head-lamps or shattered the stillness with their exhaust. Pitch black and absolute quiet held sway on the shores of Shoecraft back then.

My ten-year-old mind never questioned the fragile nature of the wonders around me. Somehow the otters, red fox, painted turtle and other wild creatures would be forever. Life would just go on as it existed in those halcyon days of pristine waters and endless woods.

The Case of the Stereophonic Squash

The volunteer squash sneaked into my garden, I assumed, under cover in the compost. Like a foreign mole in a LeCarre novel it lay hidden out of my view, entrenching itself and slyly intertwining with the other roots, ingratiating itself with the local earthworms and potato bugs. I didn't even have a hint until late May that an alien lingered in wait. It sneakily and slowly shoved up a congealed clod of rabbit droppings near my newly planted 'Fair Bianca'—a rose with white blossoms which was needed to offset all the pinks and reds that grew in proximity.

Clever. The clod of congealed rabbit dung sat there like a large floppy sun hat disguising the nefarious seedling while it grippingly entrenched itself and sucked strength from the nearby soil and plants. Poor 'Fair Bianca"—perhaps now, "weak and sickly Bianca". This earthy espionage was all taking place on a roof-top garden that served as the top and cover of my earth-bermed workshop and office.

Then one day while I was weeding around my Bianca I disturbed the disguising clod, and the tightly-tensed tendril twanged toward me like a steel spring suddenly released. I jerked my head back in an automatic reflex and almost fell, crushing a tender shoot on my new rose. Poor, poor Bianca!

I recognized the oval leaf and the thick stem for what it was, or at least for what it could become if I let it stay. And even though I stood ready to heap any blaming of Bianca's potential maiming directly on its ugly head, I felt a shadow of hesitation shade my reasoning. While in this half light I wondered what nefarious mischief this squash would wreak on Bianca's tightly-packed and pungent petals. After all, the word "squash" by its very onomatopoeic essence did not bode well. I leaned over to yank this smasher of things out of the soil, but some compelling force held my hand. In that instant it had been granted asylum.

Other matters tethered my thoughts and the squash was all but forgotten.

I watered with a drip system that only required a turn of the faucet so Bianca and the squash were out of sight. Indeed my squash had its "turn" on earth, but only at the far end of the hose. A week or so later I noticed that beautiful Bianca was in bloom. I hurried up the berm and over to the south end of the row of roses and as I bent I caught a heady and mysterious whiff of the tight, white rose, then my eyes moved slightly beyond. I saw, with alarm, a brutishly big bush. The once-narrow tendrils were now cable-like vines cascading down the south side of the dome. There was tightness in my throat.

A few weeks later I noticed several unruly vines were threatening to climb the neighbor's fence and wreak havoc in their immaculately-conceived and manicured yard. One fattish vine had even thrown itself over the front of the dome and was reaching across the mortared stone toward my office window. The wiry tendrils at its tip looked eerily like a witch's twisted fingers.

Unable to hide the concern from her voice and eyes, my neighbor asked, "Er, that huge vine...it's...it's just a squash isn't it?"

I confessed I could not give her any real assurances of its true nature. A frown creased her brow. The squash had now reached monster proportions!

Time slid and summer was kissing us good-by. The sun was getting slower on the rise as it did its northern slippery-slide down the eastern horizon. One morning I greeted the day early by walking through the dew-laden grass to gaze out over the dawn-calm lake. The sky was cloudless; the stars and the waning moon had been clearly visible during the dark. I wished the lake a good morning and a good day hoping it would be free of ear and water-rending craft so it could heal and rest. I then turned and walked past the heavily-laden (at last) Melrose apple tree toward the dome. There in the half-light loomed the squash—it had grown even more! The giant leaves were now shaped like massive fluted bowls, all pointing skyward. Then a wry and crazy image came running, crowding into mind. Were they listening, that mass of ears tuned to the stars and the moon—to the heavens above? Were they waiting patiently to hear from the sun? Suddenly I knew that a wildly wry and ludicrous deed must be done. Of course I was the candidate, the only candidate—I wouldn't dare tell anyone.

Carefully I cut the hollow stem of the longest vine containing about ten giant-cupped ears and gently inserted the hollow tube into my left ear, all the while praying that no one in the house had awakened and happened to be looking domeward. I cut another and put it in my right ear. I had stereophonic ears listening to the universe—hydroponically driven by the juices of the wild thing growing outside my office door! I imagined I could hear some of the songs of the universe, perhaps some celestial angels singing the praises of God's creations. I listened to the skies, the stars and the moon. I thought I could hear the rush of the coming sun—then the light came on in my daughter's bedroom. Fear of eternal ridicule gripped me and I abandoned my ears to the universe and opened the door to my earth-berm workshop to prepare some of my Country Living Grain Mills to ship to a dealer in Missouri. I put wheat berries in the mill's hopper and started turning the large flywheel (I test each mill by grinding by hand a cup of flour before I ship it). As I watched the fresh flour fall into the bin I marveled that the world was so full of a number of things —especially if your imagination is a little uninhibited and you have a sense of humor to match. Hmm, perhaps I had chanced upon the seed for a children's book. Yes, I think that would be quite fun!

The Otters are Coming! The Otters are Coming!

It was a breathless day in many ways. No wind, no clouds, temperature hovering just a tad over thirty. Joel brought the twins and Brandi over while he went to his company Christmas party. I had promised Brandi, last night at our family Christmas, that I would give her a ride in the kayak. She had said, "Cool," which was the ultimate accolade in her nine-year-old vocabulary. She'd only been in a boat once so she was excited about going. I wiped the slugs, spiders and residual gunk off the seats and the inside bottom of the old double kayak.

Brandi, an eager helper, carried the paddles and worked on a jammed life vest zipper while I wrestled, with some assists from Brandi, the white and orange hulk into the water. I hoisted Brandi above the cold water into the front cockpit of the kayak. She settled in easily, eagerly grasped the paddles and got into a ready position. The bow split the perfect surface of the lake and after a few sputter starts Brandi easily picked up the knack of paddling with a double-feathered paddle. She was a natural. We paddled north, in the shadow of the wooded shore, up the west bank of the lake. Sister, a little black and white terrier, raced down the Murchie's dock to do her doggie duty and bark furiously, all the while looking at the house to see if her mistress was noticing her protective efforts (she wasn't). We quietly skimmed by.

Sister's incessant yapping left a bigger wake than we did. As we rounded the shallow curve of the lake's south end the shadows dropped behind and we were suddenly covered by sun. The warmth was instant and wonderful.

As we headed up the eastern shore I spotted a large orange boat in the center of the lake with someone obviously fishing. I knew the boat; deep-hulled, with an inboard motor that was raucously loud and dirty. The owner was known for his disregard of the boating rules on the lake. He was infamous for water-skiing without an observer and powering around the lake after dark, both illegal acts.

As we kayaked by this fellow I asked him if he had caught any fish. He proceeded to tell me about all of the big ones he had caught, one over three pounds. When my eyes lit up with interest (I'd forgotten for a moment who I was talking to) and I started to paddle closer to the boat, he immediately interjected that he of course had released all of these big fish, and besides he'd caught them on other days. I steered the conversation toward speedboats on the lake and lamented that all the new housing and speedboat population had probably driven away the otters. I said that I missed them.

"Ah, but there's a pair of otters that come down the lake every morning," he smiled. "Why, they're as big as my cocker spaniel. I really like watching them play."

I wanted to believe him, but couldn't. My skepticism held my enthusiasm in reign. I hadn't seen an otter for at least two years and suddenly I was hearing a different story. As we paddled, visions of playful otters danced in my head. I recounted some of my favorite otter stories to Brandi. By the time we had circumnavigated the lake I was determined to have an otter watch starting with the next coming of the sun.

I kept a watchful otter-eye starting at seven a.m. It was still dark, with slightly hoary hints of light on the horizon. The vision was poor but there was nothing to mask the sound.

Otters are noisy eaters. You can hear them crunching their breakfasts of crawdads and fresh-water clams for the length of the lake on a still winter morning. I walked to the lake and hunkered down to listen. Was I wasting my time? Well, the otters may be a no-show, I thought, but the solitude and its attendant thoughts were grand. I pondered my family—my loving wife Ann, a conservative, bordering-on-shy, Irish girl who put up with and usually sustained my often less-than-sound projects and ideas. Ann's deep and consistent spirituality, coupled with her desire to always do better, kindled my desire to be a better husband and father. Indeed I had been blessed.

It was while I was warmly immersed in a mental baptism of blessings that I heard what I thought I would never hear again. A faint crunch floated down the lake's surface from the south end. My senses were aprickle. The otters were coming, the otters were coming! And they did! It took them awhile to work their way down the lake, but in about fifteen minutes they were slither-sliding on the Ellis' raft and noisily chomping their breakfast clams. What fun, those playful creatures! They made my morning, they made my day, and in the remembering, perhaps many more days to come. And, miracle of miracles, these joyful otters have softened my attitude towards a neighbor—which is always a good thing.

Romance Beneath the Ice

Saturday brought barely-thirtyish temperatures and dark, heavy-bottomed skies. By evening the swollen clouds began to lighten. The gray unfurled into endless cottony-white curtains that flowed and fluttered and soon began their draping of the darkling trees and the earth—a dazzling opening scene for a two-day marathon of falling, powder-fine, seamlessly-unsullied, white. The thunder-thighed clouds lost countless tons in a mere forty-eight hours (Eat your heart out, weight watchers). Heaven's loss, earth's gain!

The re-mantled earthscape was cleaner, simpler, refreshing, far more quiet. On Monday the snow clouds showed us yet another flaky side. The slimmed-down fluff said "Sayonara" and headed east when it felt the nudgings of frigid arctic air.

The skies became flawless, free. The arctic air hunkered in, harder still. By Sunday evening sleds, tubes, and anything else that was slippery and slidey had been freed from basement bondage and carport confinement and were zizzing down the hills and slopes.

The newly-created road across from our drive was soon thronging with sledders. The top-of-the-hill residents either chained up or stayed home. Several parked on the verge of our lot.

Monday and Tuesday night the arctic air truly expressed itself. This morning when I looked out of the front window I realized that indeed small numbers can be chillingly forceful. It seems a committee of seven degrees—a committee of one would have been more effective still—had provoked the lake into a change of complexion. Most of the cove had become filigreed crystal. The shoreward edge of the ice was hoary from the first night's snow, the virgin outer edge, transparent still. The newer, pristine stuff was clear enough to see the fluid lake beneath. The ice had an-chored at the shore and nibbled at the surface water until it had extended itself into a frozen shelf about thirty feet into the lake.

As I was marveling at the seemingly rapid advance of the ice in so short a time I noticed what appeared to be a school of very large fish swimming beneath the ledge of ice. Their size was breathtaking! Never had I seen so many large fish in our little lake. True, I had seen 7 and 8 pound bass in our waters, but never a school of these lunkers. I watched with awe as the big fat fish, well over a foot and a half long, swirled, then swam swiftly toward the ice's outer edge. Suddenly they popped out and bobbed to the surface of the water. Whoa!

My mind had to regroup to what I was seeing. The large, underwater school was suddenly transformed into a floating armada—an armada of Mergansers. About ten of the starkly black and white fish ducks had been scouring under the ice for a finny entrée; one had succeeded. The hapless fish was flapping furiously in the Merganser's beak. The Merganser in turn was frantically flapping his black-tipped wings and churning his webbed feet, trying to elude his ravening mates and their larcenous efforts to relieve him of his catch. Amidst much squawking and water splashing the leading Merganser jerked his neck and beak to gain the gulp at a galloping pace. ("Chew your food before you swal-low, dear.") The fingerling in turn put up a flipping good fight. But alas, he flopped when he should have flipped and suddenly he had a first-hand look at the dark side of a Merganser.

The lake continued to freeze and soon the Mergansers were no more—the ice had squeezed them out. Jaime, my fourteen-year-old, prayed for deep-freeze weather to continue. I too, thought it would be nice to have ice thick and solid enough to skate and sled on. And the sun, the glorious sun, was wonderful to see and bask in on those frost-filled, cloud-free days. But now (10th of February) not a sliver of ice or sun is to be seen. Warm temperatures, endless, fat, gray skies, and ceaseless downpours born on a southern wind came roaring in, and virtually overnight the ice is thinning as fast as my hair.

Within a day it has begun to break up. Avalanches rumbled down the mountains, and Steven's and Snoqualmie passes are impassable. Rivers are swollen and the city of Portland is deluged, streets closed, and sewers doing a reverse flush into peoples homes and into the streets. How easy for Mother Nature (I wonder how God feels about Mother Nature getting credit or blame for everything over which He has infinite control?) to bring the commerce of humankind to a standstill.

But even during the gloomy warmth wave there is beauty. The thinned ice will actually bend to the wave action. Its undulations are smooth and shiny—no small ripples in between, just a barely-bulged continuum resembling subtle, but moving, rounded hills smoothed by a million weather beaten years, and all contained within a cold and icy outer shell. At the edge, where water and crystal meet, the gale-forced ice first broke into tiny shards. As it heaved and cracked and piled upon itself, it tinkled and chirped like an aviary stuffed with a thousand birds.

On the first day while the ice was still stiff with cold the ice-calls were high in pitch. As the weather warmed the chirps sank lower down the scale, until at last they became so water-muted that only sluggish gurgles could be heard around the shores. The ice had struggled, then died, but sung a song of life while it still moved.

The Mergansers are back. So are the Cormorants. A speed-boat has already roaringly shattered the air and left an oily sheen in its wake. Two fishermen came and three beer cans stayed behind, their legacy and thanks for catching the fish the lake has succored.

The ice could have stayed a month and I would have been pleased. Still, I'll watch for the beauty. It's always there when I take the time for my senses to absorb and observe.

The Summer of ' 93

The summer of '93 in the Pacific Northwest was an unadulterated gray. The height, depth and breadth of June, July and August were various shades of almost black in every moist cranny of its ninety-two rain-sodden days. In the wry room of my mind I conjured up an eternal cumulus cover forever oozing in from outer space.

Was it some monster-clouding cloak that the Martians or the C.I.A. spewed on us so that the August orbit of the Mars probe couldn't focus on the plains of that planet to reveal the Andean-sized architecture of a human visage created by beings far more intelligent than we? (It just wouldn't do to let the masses know that in the human race we earthlings probably weren't first at the starting gate.)

My other wry, overwrought option: Mother Nature in a grand fit of grump had made "gray" her color of choice for the Pacific Northwest (Retribution for our shoddy care and keeping of her beloved earth?).

But I tried not to complain too loudly, and never with real rancor, for having lived thirty years on a small lake some fifty miles north of Seattle I had learned to tolerate, even appreciate, the usually ever-greening rains that the Pacific Northwest regularly serves up as her meteorological entree. But even though the unsummery skies of '93 forced me to swim in lake waters lurking with sixty-something warmth-sucking Fahrenheit's, I still considered anyone who got seriously nasty with their Northwest bashing ill-informed and having a shrink-wrapped mentality (all package, little product and virtually impenetrable). After all, even though we Northwesterners had slimmed and slug-riddled garden veggies, and berries bearded with hoary rot, those disasters were less than minor compared to the Midwest. Theirs were cities and farms inundated, homes and businesses destroyed. Even now, bedrooms where children once slept and lovers once snuggled are lying fetid with Mississippi mud. Chenille bedspreads and carpets of Dupont's best are slowly becoming irredeemable muck. In mid-September the Midwest rains began yet another onslaught on Midwesterners' spirits and possessions.

Some have called it the 100 year flood. Others, who watch weather patterns closely, voice an even greater fear. Between the hurricanes and unrelenting rain, human habitation through destruction alley must surely give way to desolation. And the East Coast? It sizzled and fried, then waited in uneasy anticipation for the hurricanes to start cooking on the back burners of the Atlantic.

Our Northwest curse was small in comparison, merely moldy berries, slug-riddled greens and thousands of pale bodies saved from the seeds of melanoma. Put in perspective, it was close to heaven.

On those rare days when the sun broke through the gridlock of gray it was hail and hallelujah time for me. Bathed in celestial light the verdant greenery, stockinged by cerulean bays and lakes, was so brilliant, compared to the precedent gray, that it almost hurt.

For me the 'unsummer of '93' ended on Friday the 27 of August. It was brilliant. It was beautiful. I almost cried at its intensity. Amazingly, most of September danced in the sunlight. My soul rejoiced.

Crow with a Message

I don't like crows. They are noisy, pushy, greedy, generally obnoxious and not a very pretty bird to look at. They regularly peck gaping holes in the largest, most beautiful and succulent of my apple crop. They steal food out of my dog's bowl, and they make an unearthly racket before the sun even makes a showing, with the sole intent of irritating and keeping me awake.

Crows are thoroughly rotten. Whoever came up with the appellation for a group of those raucous ravens had it right on. A murder of crows. I can't count the times that I've felt like doing exactly that. The last time I didn't count was just a week ago. I'd just washed my car when out of a bower of maple trees behind our home burst a black demon crow announcing every foot of his flight with ear-rending, ratchety caws. Yes, of course, he was on a bombing run.

As I scrubbed and hosed the freshly-splatted droppings from my windshield and hood, my mind churned with ways to bring about the demise of about thirty crows. No, not thirty, thirty thousand—that should take care of at least a ten-mile radius around my home. That would be something to crow about. A shotgun sounded appealing, but I didn't own one. Poison in the dog food? But then I had visions of Max, my shepherd, with all four legs sticking straight up like a furry four-poster. No, poisoned food wouldn't do. A blowgun with curare (strychnine from strychnos toxifera vine) tipped darts...hmmm neat, but what if I sucked in by mistake? And hiring some Amazonian natives to patrol my woods seemed out of the question—besides, they are probably unionized and wouldn't work for anything less than three shrunken heads an hour. Then I contemplated stocking my wooded lot with tree-climbing snakes. I'd heard that birds head for other climes when they see a python slithering down the branch toward them. Wouldn't you?

Just as my mental foment was reaching a froth I heard a strange and forlorn call. It had a soft, mellow sadness like a lovelorn serenade to the moon. It seemed to be emanating from high atop our huge old fir tree. I heard it once again, "kwaaa, kwaaa...!" Something rare and exotic, I thought—an eagle, a peregrine, an osprey, or perhaps something uncatalogued by man. But watch and wait as I would, I saw nothing but raucous crows and a robin and a wren or two.

Suddenly a murder of about forty crows went winging overhead. They cast a heavy shadow over the ground. The sight of so many sent a shiver through me. It reminded me of a deadly plague blotting out the sun. I hated the crows and was positive that they had frightened away my rare and lovely "kwaaa" bird.

After a year of not knowing, the revelation came. I was swimming north along the western shore of the lake on an early, marvelously sunny morning. The speedboats were still at rest, no belching and churning pistons to disturb the extraordinary peace! As I swam I heard the long drawn, "kwaaa, kwaaa". It came in pairs, occasionally in triplets. The alder, fir, and cedar trees were bathed in a marvelous light—perhaps I could see the source. Nothing! Nothing but a solitary crow in a half-dead alder. Drat! All I needed was a black blotch to mar my morning swim. As I swam the crow launched from the limb and flapped to keep up with me. He flew twenty or so yards ahead, found a branch with a vantage point, and waited. He was watching me and I was watching him. Then he did an extraordinary thing; he dipped his head and neck in a long, and I begrudgingly admit, graceful swoop, and as he did the silence was delicately parted with a beautiful drawn-out "kwaaa".

As I watched he repeated it. Each 'kwaaa' was about two seconds long—soft, forlorn; I perceived a touch of pathos. He followed me down the length of the lake and each time he perched he did his graceful bow and presented me on the palette of early-morning gold his twin "kwaaas". I couldn't help myself, but each time he "kwaaed" I smiled. He knew I was listening. I knew that he knew that a grumpy, biased and bigoted human would at least have the chance to have one rusty-hinged door of his mind pried slightly ajar. I opened my mouth and did my best to imitate his "kwaaa" just so he would know that the message was received.

Where Have All the Fathers Gone?

My daughter, one of five, came in the door and dumped all of her school books on the kitchen table. Before I could even object to her aeronautical maneuvers (pile it here, pile it there, pilot everywhere) she announced, "Dad, I'm a minority."

"Oh?" ("Oh" is my euphemism for *not having a clue.*)

"Yeah, they took a poll in C.W.I. (Current World Issues) and there were only four of us out of a class of 27 that still had their real dads living with them."

"Wow!" My "Wow" carried the seeds of depression.

"Where did all the fathers go?" I asked.

"I dunno. Maybe instead of real dads they were real duds!"

Having taken a few lumps in the past for making blanket condemnations or commendations, I reached for some middle ground.

"Well, you know it takes two people working together, making sacrifices co-equally, to really make a go of marriage."

"Ok, so why aren't the dads still there working and sacrificing?"

My mouth was open but the words weren't there.

My daughter noticed the lapse, kissed me on the cheek and said: "It's okay, Dad, you don't have to make excuses for someone else's father. I really appreciate you and Mom for being good parents and hanging in there."

Well, I appreciated her appreciation—even to the point of my vision getting a little misty. With the emotion came a thought, which I voiced. "Maybe it's the lack of role models. People just aren't being taught, either by precept or example, what a good parent or spouse really is. Take a look at the media. Who's glorified and publicized the most?"

"Magic Johnson," she replied, without missing a beat (he was a sports figure currently big in the news), "for being so true, noble, and forthright in coming out of the closet with his AIDS problem." She pointed her finger toward her open mouth and gave a gagging sound. We'd both noted that buried in a couple of the "Magic" news stories was the fact that the basketball star was a flagrant womanizer. How many young girls and women had Magic contaminated with the virus of death? No one seemed to be counting. They were too busy fawning over a superstar. Noble, true and forthright indeed! His wife and any future children he might dare have will be hard-pressed to appreciate those "Magic moments".

Off the top of our heads my daughter and I, in rapid-fire remembrance, named politicians, entertainers, born-again evangelists and even a local school teacher as those currently bannered in the media for conduct that I knew had surely twisted and mangled the circle of their family unity and trust. Their wives and tender-hearted children, without question, were being emotionally devastated.

Chins in our hands, my daughter and I looked morosely at each other across the table. She suddenly brightened. "What if you had a chance to talk to all the men in world, say for five minutes or less, what would you tell them? No matter what their background—Jew, Baptist, Atheist, Buddhist, Muslim, whatever!"

"And what I tell them, in five minutes or less, is going to give them the key to being a great father and a super husband. Right?"

She nodded, yes, while I frantically searched my memory bank. "Okay", I said, "but remember, this will be only a key. It won't change lives or give men a joyful relationship with their wives or children unless they use the key and keep turning it in what has to be some very rusty locks."

"All right, let's have it." She said impatiently.

"Ta da!" I gave a little drum roll on the tile table-top.

"Men, be the head of your family...!"

"Wooh!" she interrupted, "That's going to draw some heavy flack from Sarah" (a feminist-leaning friend).

"Ah, you may not have noticed, daughter dear, but I think I was cut off before I even got out of the starting gate. Perhaps if you'd let me finish I might say something that even Sarah will approve of."

"Well, maybe. But some women would go absolutely ballistic at the idea of a having a man tell them what to do."

"But what I'm suggesting is just the opposite of a dictatorship! If you'd let me back up and get another start I think you'll understand."

"Okay Papa San. My lips are sealed." With that she gave a zipping motion across her mouth.

"Men, be the head of your families!" My daughter's eyebrows elevated toward her hairline. I raised a palms-out restraining hand. Her lips only twitched, but didn't part—admirable restraint.

I continued, "Men, be the head of your families in patience!"

Her eyebrows rose again, this time with the beginning of understanding. I forged ahead. "Men, be the head of your families in tenderness. Men, constantly be concerned about and work on being the head of your family in forgiveness, in kindness, in courtesy, in consideration, in respect, and in all other virtues. Be the head of the family in devotion and loyalty. Men, if you do that, I think wives will find it easy to take on the same responsibilities."

With that I drew a deep breath, looked at my watch and said: "I think that's about it, in barely over a minute."

My daughter sat mentally digesting. Finally after about a minute of silence she asked, "Did you come up with that yourself?"

"No," I admitted, "I had to be taught—had to learn it. Then I had to practice it so it would become mine. And, as you well know, it's still not entirely mine—so I'll still keep working, practicing and learning, if that's okay with you?"

"Dad, I'll be your guinea pig for practicing forgiveness, kindness, courtesy, and consideration any day!" A sly little smile came to her lips. She cleared her throat: "Papa San, you know the right front fender of your car?"

"Of course I know the fender of my car!" I blustered.

"Well, it's aged a little—you know, a wrinkle here and there."

I worked on getting a grip, reached back in time and remembered, "A car is only a thing. A *thing* is transitory, momentary at best. Your children are forever." I wrestled momentarily with reality, mentally reached into my limited view of eternity then asked, "You're okay, you weren't hurt?"

"No, I'm just fine." She smiled. I smiled too—thankful for all those Sundays past when I listened to and felt what was being taught.

Uncommon Commotion

I delight in seeing my children talk, laugh, work and play with each other. When they're all together there's an uncommon commotion of voices and movement not unlike ocean surf muted by distance and a dune or two. Strangely, instead of being an irritant it gives me an enormous sense of pleasure to be in a space gently aroar with family—for that roar has been, almost always, aglow with warm hues of love.

This happy communion, whether reading aloud from good books, sharing life's stories or horsing around to test physical or mental prowess, seems more and more to imbue me with a halcyon feeling of swimming effortlessly in a warm azure sea where all the fish are dolphin-friendly and the yellow sun has only gentle rays.

Often, when my family gathers round I imagine, no—stronger than that—I feel myself gliding through an ocean endless in warmth and peace, and I have no doubt that this a small and delicious taste of what God wishes for his children—for all eternity.

Come See the Bubbles from the Sky!

It was 11:30 p.m. when I went outside to check on Max and say good night to him. As it turned out Max wasn't in his dog-house, and I walked to the end of the porch and stepped out from the protection of the roof onto the sidewalk so I could look at the sky and see what hope there was, if any, for a rainless weekend. The floodlight on the side of the house was beaming into the darkness and it illumined an extraordinarily fine mist. The beam reflected back what appeared as tiny specks of white gently floating toward the earth.

As I stared into the night I noticed that the mist was composed of a mixture. Two types of precipitation reflected back from the aureole of light. It was a delightful dawning when I realized that at least 60 percent of the mist was composed of bubbles, tiny bubbles probably not much bigger than the effervescence coming from a carbonated drink. I actually saw some of them spontaneously burst as they floated randomly toward the earth.

I blinked my eyes, thinking that I must be seeing things. I had never heard or read that a light, floaty, fine mist could be bubbles. Had Lawrence Welk died and made an effervescent entrance through the pearly gates? Could the 500 watt porch lamp deceive me? I was sure I could see tiny spherical walls on the transparent orbs that floated ever so gently toward my face. As I stared in awe at the fizz's downy drift, unmoved by any breeze, I realized that interspersed between the buoyant mini-spheres were thread-thin, arrow-straight streaks of light. The streaky blurs, I thought, must be the solid drops, the rain, albeit very fine, plummeting down.

For several minutes I stood with my face upturned seeing if I could feel the difference between the streakers and the floaters on my cheek and forehead. I could—the watery little streakers greeted my upturned face with a hint of sting and the floaters? An imperceptible kiss as they burst against my skin.

Excitedly I called Jaime, our 14-year-old to "Come, see the bubbles from the sky!"

She rolled her eyes and gave me her now much-practiced, "Why do you take up my precious time with your crazy ideas" stare, but reluctantly came with me to the end of the porch. She gave the ever so gentle and refreshing mist about four seconds of her valuable teen-time and declared, "Nothing has ever been said in my science class about mist being bubbles. They're not bubbles, it's just fine rain." She turned on her heel and stridently tromped off the porch into the house. The door slammed, an exclamation mark for her "no bubbles" pronouncement.

I stayed and marveled at the bubbles that "couldn't exist" for another five minutes or so—the solid streaks like confetti and the bubbles like champagne fizz. All in all a celebration for my senses. I felt sorry for the science class that knew so much. Give them time and maybe they'll be blessed with the wonderful knowledge that they really know so very, very little.

Later, after I went to bed, I told Ann that I had just witnessed something that perhaps no one else in the world may have seen. I explained my mini miracle to her and she squeezed my hand and said, "I'm glad you saw the effervescent rain, what a delightful thing. Next time the soft mist comes I'd like to see the bubbles."

It's nice to have at least one person believe in your personal miracles, even though they are very, very small—and perhaps not even what you think they are at all.

We Three for Eternity!

When I got up at 5:30 this morning I found Alison in the living room breast-feeding six-day-old Emily. Alison looked tired; she'd fed Emily at midnight, at 2:30 and at a nudge past five. Never once through the night did I hear Emily make a peep. The reason, I suspect, is that Alison feels it might put a small dent in her mantle-of-motherhood if Emily fussed or cried for even a nanosecond or two. Alison's bed-to-crib speed must be sonically super. They'll both learn.

The added stress of getting their accumulations moved into our basement before James starts student teaching at Granite Falls high school (a non-paying but obligatory step in getting your teaching certificate) had pushed Alison close to tears.

I asked if I could hold the baby. The answer was yes. Emily fussed and squirmed lying in my lap, so I rested her on my chest and shoulder and began to gently pat her on the back. Such a small back! Two fingers lightly tapping seemed sufficient on her tiny baby frame. Alison moved closer and rested her head on my shoulder next to Emily while I continued gently patting, patting, lightly tapping on Emily's baby back. A mini burp arose and Emily's fussiness evaporated with it. Pat, pat, pat—tap, tap, tap: three generations joined in gentle rhythm and harmony. We three for eternity—Emily, Alison and me.

A week or so later I was feeling a little downish. Alison came up to me smiling and holding Emily. Alison leaned over and kissed me on the cheek and said, "Thanks for having me Dad, so I could have Emily." I saw the adoration, the happiness, the peace, the love, and I was down no more. I recognized the circle. Indeed, "Men are that they might have joy!"

Masters of Remembrance

I watched as they tagged a hatchery-raised Coho salmon, a smolt (smoltification: a change that turns all the young salmon's instincts and drive toward salt water) and released it. With barely a moment's hesitation the tiny salmon swam through the newly-opened gate of the hatchery pond into the adjacent creek. It seemed driven as though it knew that it was destined for much bigger things. Some species of salmon spend up to three years in the fresh water; others, such as our small Coho, hurriedly and relentlessly work their way through rocks and rills, treacherous rapids, even down thunderous waterfalls in their sea-quest.

Predators are legion—man, birds, animals, pollution, voracious fish—all are unmerciful. The toll is great. Only a small fraction of the hatched salmon live to swim the endless sea. And the Pacific isn't exactly a place of respite for our salmon. It would appear that the river trip was merely a testing, a toughening, a schooling, so our salmon might better survive the sea and the rest of the journey. Some salmon, once they reach the vast Pacific, swim thousands of miles out into its depths. There the predators are larger—much larger. That any creature could survive this treacherous, often multi-thousand-mile journey seems miraculous to me. But we've only seen the first half of the journey, the "leaving". The "remembrance", or passage home, when contrasted with the "leaving", that is truly miraculous!

When the salmon receives that inner call to return to its beginnings, the great host of annihilators still lie in wait—with some extra heavy-weights thrown in. This time our salmon is returning to a minuscule spot, a mere dot compared to its first goal, the sea.

There are theories, of course, of what forces guide our finny friend home: polar magnetism? Smell? We humans tend to relegate this homeward pull to something our captive minds can comprehend. (Captive to those things we think we know and understand.) In stark truth our telestial reasoning can't possibly comprehend the powerful beacon that guides our salmon home. Its compelling strength is beyond imagination.

Consider this: going home is all uphill; no resting; no floating; no going with the flow. Pausing means going backwards. Once fresh water is reached there is no eating. The drive to reach the primal asylum obviates hunger. The struggle upward has to be made on reserves—reserves stored away especially for this trial.

The call to return is so powerful that only death or disability keep the salmon from reaching home. Some salmon, within mere yards of their birthing spot, have encountered a screen. Observers have noted that the salmon will batter, no matter the cost to themselves, against the screen that separates them from home until the mesh gives way.

In the vernacular of computerese, geneticists claim that the salmon are hard-wired to return home.

I've heard both poet, prophet, and paragons of science proclaim essentially the same for we humans. Wordsworth said it well: "Our birth is but a sleep and a forgetting /Our life star hath elsewhere its setting and cometh from afar/ Not in utter nakedness, not in entire forgetfulness/ But trailing clouds of glory we come from God who is our home."

The Epilady Epicenter

While rummaging through a closet I chanced on an old ad from the eighties for an Israeli-built gadget touted as the ultimate in hair removal. In reality it was the ultimate torture device, dubbed by some as "Israel's revenge."

I remember well that our daughter had dropped the birthday hint several times, "An Epilady would be nice." But I knew the price wasn't so nice. Around seventy-five dollars, initially. Eventually we found one for twenty-nine dollars. However, a foreboding sense of doom descended when the check-out clerk said, "My mother cried when she used her Epilady."

Since there were nine people in line behind us, and scene—making seemed unseemly...we paid and left. But the phrase, "My mother cried," weighed heavily.

Once home, the Epilady was plugged in, "Ouch!" Was my daughter's first utterance. "It's like being shocked!" Was her second. "I don't understand," she said, "the demonstrator ran it over my palm and there was no pain."

"Well, there wouldn't be unless you have hairy palms," I suggested.

My daughter finally steeled herself to the pain and set about snagging leg hair. Fifteen minutes later she had depilatated a whole two square inches. Why, it shouldn't take over three hours of pain to Epilate one pair of legs.

My son figured it would take about a month to trim the lawn with it, but at least we wouldn't hear the grass cry. When my daughter returned it, the clerk wryly smiled and said, "Thanks."

"Why are you thanking me?" My daughter asked.

"Because some customers don't hand it back, they throw it at me."

In retrospect the Epilady certainly won't receive the Jenkins'
"Good Mousekeeping Squeal of Approval."

The Car Conspiracy

As our children grew older, so did their away-from-home involvement. The eternal chauffeuring of our children became very taxing and taxiing indeed.

As their interests expanded, we found ourselves constantly car-ing up and down the roads to schools, church, basketball, football, track, drama, friends' houses, and to jobs. The list went on and on. Our car never cooled. It was truly a hot rod.

Mom and Dad's Taxi Service began to weigh more and more heavily on our time and budget, I found myself wistfully longing for the day when my children would be old enough to drive—joy of joys—even have their own cars! I even imagined the spare time I would have for my projects.

Well, years have passed and part of my dream has come true. Three of my children now have their own cars. Now I can retire my "Dad's Taxi Service" sign? Right? Wrong! You see, I have just spent the better part of a week and a half with bleeding knuckles and grime-ground hands replacing a blown head gasket in my daughter's Mazda. I almost blew my own gasket in the process. Prior to that my other daughter rolled her Plymouth Horizon on a rain-slick curve. She was only shaken, but the sun will never rise over that Horizon again.

That mess only took a month to straighten out, so to speak. Not long before that my son's old Toyota threw a rod, and just prior to that—well, you get the picture.

Now the sign says, "Dad's Car Repair Service".

Personal projects? Well, maybe some other decade.

Moldy Malediction

The people who blather on about global warming obviously haven't experienced that moldy malediction that the Pacific Northwesterners call summer. Cloud-gloomed summers do not good vacations make. It's not as much fun swimming under a chilly, clouded sky as it is when the clear azure heavens let old Sol blaze in from on high. And the tomatoes don't ripen as fast, or they don't ripen at all. Probably the most galling part of a summer without sun is that it just doesn't seem like summer. How dull.

Anti-perspirant makers must curse the clouded excuses of summer that are often proffered up in the Pacific Northwest. We have more goose-bumps than sweat. Of course, sun-slim Northwest summers don't cause universal loathing. Slugs absolutely adore cool dampness. Those little slimers have reproductive heydays during the gloom and drizzle of Northwest numbness. Each slug is capable of thousands of new hatchlings. And if you cock your ear groundward, you'll hear the hoorahs of twenty-billion slugs celebrating the gloom. However, a more pleasant plus of coolness crops up—tender strawberries.

You see, my berry patch is awesomely tricked into thinking cool spring has arrived again. Delicate white blossoms festoon my plants in August, and just the other day I picked a handful of big, luscious, red strawberries and brought them in to Ann. As I type this story, strawberry essence wafts up from my palms—a reminder that a sunless summer is not all bad.

Six-Year-Olds, Chocolate Chip Cookies, and Carnage

There's no question that the most delicious chocolate-chip cookies in the world are baked by six-year-olds, if you ignore a few minor details.

Patience must certainly be a heavenly attribute. After all, you see so little of it displayed on earth. But to parents, who patiently teach their children how to cook—to those intrepid souls must go some saintly seal of honor. For instance, my twelve-year-old is a formidable cookie baker. Her output is prodigious. Sometimes seven, eight, nine dozen at a time. The counter is jammed with cookie sheets, mixing bowls, egg shells, beaters, cartons. The floor becomes a horizontal version of fly paper.

Some of her earlier tries were less than palatable. But we oohed and aahed anyway. Then after she went to bed, I buried them in the compost.

Lately the floors definitely aren't as sticky, and now her cookies are absolutely delicious. They're inhaled in a whiffle unless hidden in very secret places.

The other day, under Ann's supervision, our six-year-old spread her culinary wings a little further and Ann was letting her hold an electric beater. Ann left the kitchen just for a moment, and as I peered in, batter was flying wildly—spattering on walls and windows.

No, it wasn't accidental. Our six-year-old had her mouth open wide and was catching the galluptuous globs of batter as they flew by. As I rushed to stop the carnage, some batter hit me on the lips. Mmm, you know, flying chocolate chips aren't all that bad.

Orville, Wilbur, and the Flying Cat

The Soviets attempted to wrong some of the rights. The Wright *Brothers*, that is, by claiming that Orville's success at Kitty Hawk was actually preceded by a Russian. All right, Mr. Gorbachev, if that's your game, wait 'til you hear *my* kitty hawk story. It'll really give you "paws" for thought.

I'll admit my airborne hero bears an unlikely name—Shadow. My children found him hungry and crying, so they brought him up to our deck to keep the dogs from harming him. He was fed and coddled. The whole family delighted in watching his tireless antics. Shadow, as you have guessed by now, was a kitten, and he especially loved a grocery bag. He would leap inside the bag and it would jerk and flip like a Mexican jumping bean.

Well, one day the wind started gusting up—forty miles an hour we later learned. Shadow was in cat heaven playing with that wind-blown animated bag. Then in one marvelous and simultaneous moment, both gust and kitten swept into the bag. It became airborne and catapulted over the rail. For one lofty moment, I saw shadow's flying saucer-like eyes glazed in wonderment, then he plummeted ten feet to terra firma. I found him dazed, but unhurt. His heart was pounding a tattoo through his skin. I wanted to name him Hawk to honor Orville, but my children would have none of my puns.

I did, however, get one last groan. As the peaceful cat lay gently rumbling in my arms, I quipped that he would make a purrfect pilot for some 'hairline' or other.

A Meal Fit for a King

One of our family's favorite cartoons shows a man seated at the table with a plate of food in front of him. The caption says, "This meal is fit for a king! Here, King!"

And then there are meals that aren't even fit for King.

I like to cook, and when Ann is sick or away I get to move into the kitchen with free abandon. However, my culinary capers are not always greeted with enthusiasm. My children are full of suspicions. Their suspicions are somewhat justified, for I have been known to slip in some wild, wayside weeds—all edible, of course—or to lace lasagna with some healthful brewer's yeast or something. If I'm subtle enough to evade their suspicious minds, the meal goes down easily enough. But once discovered or imagined, kiss the meal goodbye—they treat it and me like the plague. I've noticed in the family prayer on those days there's an extra fervency in pleading that their mother will get well very soon.

The final blow came several weeks ago. Even before I finished preparing it, I had suspicions that my casserole would be a flop. It would never pass muster at the table. So to avoid another public embarrassment, I quickly dumped it into the dog's bowl. Well, the rudest blast of all came when Max wouldn't even sniff it! He just cocked an ear in the general direction of his bowl. After several moments, his ear wilted like a tired flower, then he walked away. I carried the bowl of rejection to where Max sat with a look of benign, or was it canine, repugnance stamped on his furry mug.

I explained that if my children saw his rejection I'd be teased to derisive oblivion. He listened, I saw his nose twitch; hope rose, then Max turned on his heels (four of them) and retreated into the woods.

So much for man's best friend!

When I dumped the casserole into the compost, I turned and ran. I couldn't stand to see another rejection.

Teenage Geese

By October the water can cool to a point where swimming ceases to be fun, and since my hypothermia encounter of a close kind (I passed out in the shower after a January swim in an ice-fringed lake) I had stopped pushing beyond the chill to go swimming. After that scare I reluctantly admitted to myself that doing the polar bear routine was endangering my physical fitness more than enhancing it. I couldn't stay in frigid water long enough to get any aerobic exercise. I could literally feel the heat being sucked out, particularly from my head, and I suspect that all I was doing was establishing, at least in my mind, macho marks in some dubious numb-skull hall of fame.

Fortunately this year we'd had a relatively balmy October. Monday the lake was quiet, no speed boats to maim and destroy, and the sun was gleaming on the water. The night-time temperature had dipped below forty on only two nights. The lure of swimming tugged mightily.

I waded into the definitely-chilling water and started swimming north along the western shore, and as I came out of the cove there, waiting just around the bend, was a gaggle of goggle-eyed Canadian geese. They were agitated with my intrusion. I couldn'tblame them—something big and ugly was swimming directly toward them.

One of the geese made a strange, throaty noise—those geese had an abundance of neck to get throaty with—probably a warning to stay out of their way.

They veered to one side as if to let me by. I said, "Thank you," and tried to make other comforting sounds as I swam on past. Their eyes never left me. As I stroked by I realized that these were young geese, probably the equivalent of teenagers, but I wasn't sure. They were lean, trim, and youthful looking.

I continued talking to them as I swam, and to my delight they began following me. The creamy-white markings on their upper throat made them look like young maidens with tight, white chin straps—making sure no wrinkles or sags developed to mar their graceful lines. They started inching closer and I began to wonder if they weren't eyeing me as a prospective meal—or at least, more optimistically, someone who might proffer one somewhere along the line. It was then that I noticed that the tiny black feathers that swathed their long and elegant necks had a slightly rough and crinkly look that, for all the world, had the appearance of black crepe paper wrapped tightly around their pole-like necks.

They followed me all the way to the southern tip of the lake, sometimes keeping abreast, sometimes falling behind and pursuing a deviant course, but always coming back When I turned and headed for home they hesitated, then as one they arced through the placid lake to follow. The ten of us formed a strange armada, I the strangest of them all, as we swam the shores of Shoecraft. The nine proper maidens, mostly feathers and air, fairly skimmed the water's shell while I, with my equatorial rotundity, sank beneath with great abundanty. I must have evoked a humorous sight in the eyes of those young geese. I could have sworn that I heard them tittering as we swam. Certainly there couldn't be anything more fun than a giggling gaggle of geese.

When I got to the shore they loitered. I went to the house and found a jar of lentils.

"Wholesome stuff for geese," I thought, and went back to broadcast a few on the beach.

The more curious of the nine came ashore and pecked cautiously. They didn't peck for long. They made some hissy, grumbly noises, pulled up their chin straps, stuck their bills in the air and tromped back into the water. These geese were not big on lentils. They reminded me of my daughters! Then I had an idea. I ran to the house and came back as quickly as I could before they could wander too far. I cast my new offering on the troubled waters. Two geese approached—it was gone in a whiffle. There was an electricity—not just ripples, but waves were made as all nine rushed and bumped to shore. No more Miss Nice—the chin straps were loosed, the beaks were bared, they hissed and shoved and gobbled and pecked. My offering was gone in seconds.

I looked down at the empty wrappers in my hand and slowly wadded them into a ball for simpler carrying. As the carton crumpled the smell of stale french fries and a segment of an uneaten burger assailed my nose. No question, those birds were teenagers-through and through.

Time after Time

Dates and time often didn't seem important enough for me to make remembering a priority, particularly when I was younger. Events stand out like a sudden moon on a rain-swept night, but as to the specific time of their occurrence—well, the best I can say is something vague like, "I think that was in the sixties...or was it the early seventies?"

Those who like things secure and tied down to rock-solid specifics are surely frustrated, or worse, with me. To me the event or the retelling of the event is the all-in-all. If a date is absolutely relevant to the story then I'll do my best to verify and specify, but usually those timely details seem elusive and ephemeral, and once again the story becomes larger than the clock or calendar that tries to tie it to some worldly frame.

And speaking of a *worldly frame*, I have a suspicion that both hard-core evolutionists and creationists would fare much better if they would throw away the clock and calendar. After all, time is only an earthly phenomenon (God and Einstein agree) and perhaps in the open frame of timelessness there would be enough space for both concepts to be examined with minds as broad as eternity itself.

The Great Escape

If your eyesight gets fuzzy and blurred, don't despair. It might be a very petty problem.

When the problems of the world seem particularly weighty and my cup of discouragement is close to overflowing, I try my great escape.

It doesn't last long, and I don't go far. I just slip out our side door in the evening and wander along a leafy path to an old dock our neighbors have. Some of the planks are a little spongy, but what a peaceful place to contemplate. I stretch my body out on the musty boards and watch the scroll of heaven unfold. To see the constellations' procession pass in perfect order and then stare beyond to the numberless galaxies always fills me with a strange mixture of peace and awe.

One such evening two of my children asked to come along. No problem, I thought. What nicer thing to share than God's vast creations? What I hadn't counted on was the ever-growing size of my entourage.

As we left the house a German shepherd stray, known only as "Boy" followed along. Our number was four. As we reached the dock we noticed, pussyfooting through the shadows, Marmalade, our cat, and his consort, Jelly Bean. Our heaven-gazing party now equaled six.

Divinely supine, I tried to point out to the children a star here, a constellation there, but my vision began to fuzz as our pets all vied for attention and warmth. A nudge here, a purr there, a furry tail lapped across my face. But the last lick was when our new-found canine decided that it was all tongue on cheek and started lapping my face.

My vision was not only blurry and furry, I was also seeing red. I bellowed the animals off the dock and gathered the children round for a few minutes of heaven gazing, unfettered by petty problems.

Becoming a Master Builder

My thumb still throbs with remembered pain from that summer of decision. The decision may seem pretty piddly to those skilled with hammer and saw—those of you who swiftly and surely measure and cut those sheets of wooden ply. But me? I can measure once, twice, and even thrice, and as surely as babies cry, my boards are sometimes too long, but most often they are way too shy.

So there I was with barely a skill at my command, having committed (for the third time) to my children that I would build them a tree house. Filled with renewed resolve and bathed in the shiny, eager gaze of those who knew that their father couldn't fail, I shinnied up our cedar tree. With hammer clutched tightly, and nails between my teeth, I shakily ascended the tree, seeking a limb for security.

I was whaling away at that nail and two-by-six when I felt that twiggy branch bend and start to give way. I had to give that nail one last great lick... and as I pounded home, it made me sick. My thumb was where the nail should have been. My children stood wide-eyed as their infallible father plummeted to the ground and writhed in agony.

As the children gathered round and inquired as to my good health I could read in their faces that they were also inquiring about the health of the tree house. Well, I knew what I had to do, and despite pulsing throbs and a purple thumb, the tree house, of sorts, was finished that day. And, I became a master builder—at least in the eyes of three young children.

Thumbing my Nose at Jean Nate' and Faberge

Nobody knows what my nose knows, at least it seems that nobody in the world of haute monde does (Haute monde is the fancy name for those cool enough to pay sixty dollars an ounce for perfume). I don't care how fancy or sex-laden their ads are, they still haven't come up with the right stuff when it comes to concocting a really ambrosial perfume.

Oh, I've done my share of sniffing at the costly cosmetic counters, but I've stopped even going into department stores since one of the haute clerks tried to charge me five dollars for inhaling too deeply. What is the real essence (I guess you could say) of my aromatic amblings? Simply this: some of the most costly perfumes have about as much appeal as being trapped in a chicken coop on a hot day.

Oh, I know that they are supposed to be super, hush-hush formulas of crushed petals and ambergris (that's whale barf to you and me), but they all miss the mark by a mile of marigolds when they are compared to the freshest, sweetest, most sensual, headiest, heaven-sent essence of all—the smell of clothes that have been hung outside to dry on a frost-filled sunny day. The aroma of sun and wind-scrubbed sheets, shirts, and pants will never be matched by any consortium of science. Mere mortals can't do it. The essence emitted from frost and wind-dried clothes was conceived in heaven. It tingles all of the senses to heights unknown by the grosser commercial stuff.

Sorry Emeraude and Chanel, but if some wintry day you chance by and see a man a-waltzing through the hoar-frost grass with stiff long-johns hugged close to cheek and nose, stop and chat. I'll tell you what the essence of life is all about.

The Woodpile

I realize that firewood is coming under fire, so to speak, from environmentalists, but honestly, my most pollution-free memories are kindled by the wood in my back yard.

My oldest daughter was home from college, and despite the number of teens (who are usually going in all directions) in our household, we found ourselves with a minor Monday-evening miracle on our hands. Everyone was going to be home at the same time. No cheerleader practice, no volleyball or basketball. No play practice and no Scout projects. Unbelievable.

My suggestion of splitting and stacking firewood as a family project was greeted with a few initial grimaces, but enthusiasm warmed at the suggestion of a cool treat at completion. So firewood and ice cream were the order of the evening. Jason and I manned the mauls and started splitting. The girls and Ann wedged wood in the cart and hauled and stacked. Joel, our oldest, was missing, but asking him to fly from the East Coast to split wood would have been a bit much, even though his zeal as a wood splitter easily equaled Conan beating back a hoard of horrific Huns.

As we stacked the freshly-split wood in the cart, Amy marveled over the beauty of the newly-revealed white alder that had fingers of red mahogany color painted in by seeping spring rains. The loading of the cart evoked in the children's minds the times I'd packed them in the cart and careened and giggled them down the road. We laughed and reminisced as the woodpile grew, and I'm sure the bonds and boundaries of our family did too.

Conversation with a Four-Year-Old

I've heard people begrudge spending too much time with children because it wasn't intellectually stimulating. Could be. But I've heard child-proffered pearls that to me far outshine the age and intellect-polished sophistries of the world.

The other day I took my four-year-old daughter, Jaime, on a three-mile walk. It turned out she only walked three-quarters of a mile and rode on my shoulders the rest of the way. While atop my shoulders she began taking an interest in my thinning hair. After a few moments she asked, "How does your hair stay in your head?" I allowed that it was roots, like trees have underground, that held my hair in, but that some of my roots were getting tired and not holding on. She thought about that a moment, then she innocently asked, "Does that mean you have lots of holes in your head?"

I wryly admitted that, yes, that was probably true. That satisfied her for a moment. Then her mind soared on to things loftier than the holes in my head. "Daddy," she asked, "Where does Heavenly Father live?"

"Why, er, in heaven," I lamely responded.

"No, where does he live?" She insisted.

I quickly launched into a heady little talk about the universe and the galaxies and how they were all circling around one grand and central point, and that God probably resided there.

"No, daddy," she impatiently said. "He lives in a big house that's bright and yellow like the sun." "I remember it," she solemnly added.

"Do you really remember it, honey?" I gently queried.

She shook her blonde little head in a firm affirmative, and I questioned no more. After all, the years she's had in which to forget her former home are only four. Mine are much, much more.

Sizzling Sun and Other Summer Silliness

Shaped by the breath of wind and tide,
Bleached and mellowed by the gaze of the sun
Burnished and grained by gentle sands,
Sea charms; tiny children of the sea

Having taken a morning drive, Ann and I eventually came to a quiet beach overlooking a bay filled with fishing boats. It was so pleasant that we grabbed some reading material and a notepad and found a log to sit on.

Our peace and solitude was short-lived. With the advent of noon the numbers grew. A man in his fifties seemed to be the presiding high priest of a growing retinue of sun worshippers. His badge of authority was skin brown beyond brown. It was beyond what my home-town leather tannery could produce with the best of dyes. He seemed to dispense beach and tanning rights with a sort of papal wave of the arm. He had even arranged the driftwood in such a manner as to allow him to form a communal clique of sun seekers. The cop on the beat even stopped to pay him homage.

By 12:30 the beach was beginning to look like strawberries at the bottom of the basket—jammed, and a little seedy. Spray bottles appeared like magic and you could hear the "shee shee" everywhere.

A girl a mere two feet from us incessantly sprayed her body. The mist kept drifting over onto my note pad. Curious, I finally asked. "Excuse me, but does the mist speed up tanning or something?"

She glared at my intrusion into her private tanning salon, then said, "Of course not. It just cools you off!" Her sunscrunched eyes then critically raked over our amply clothed bodies.

So amidst the hiss of water and the sizzle of skin, Ann and I carefully stepped around and through the bodies littering the beach—and left.

The timing was right, for within minutes we had become minorities. Suddenly it had become a sin not to be showing most of your skin.

The Primal Knead

I remember when my mom gave me fifteen cents to run three blocks and get a loaf of bread at the corner grocery. Now I have to walk five blocks to find the bread—after I'm in the store.

Never in my little-boy mind did I dream of the high adventure awaiting the adult me while shopping for that lowly loaf of bread. I should have known better than to go into a store with the name of Mega Cosmic Foods. I mean, mega and cosmic are bigger than life, my life anyway. So when the sliders opened and a swoosh of air grabbed me, I knew I'd been sucked into a black hole of retailing that far exceeded the bounds of my meager experience.

Wrong! It was a white hole, lit by green fluorescence. Before me stretched ranks of checkout stands manned, or personned, I should say—to be politically correct—by an endless chorus line of blondes whose lipstick glowed lavender in the tube light. Food cases were stacked Himalayan high in forever rows. I cricked my neck upward to see leaning towers of Gerber's strained carrots reaching to the ceiling. My palms sweated at the thought of being trapped in that canyon of cans should even a two point tip the Richter scale.

But bread! I couldn't find the bread! I finally stumbled to a consumer-friendly computer terminal and feverishly typed in the word "bread". Out of a small vent wafted the aroma of hot sourdough and a voice said, "You're now smelling today's blue-light special."

"Where?" I yelled.

The cyber-mechanical voice intoned, "Coordinate longitude on grid and proceed to northeast quadrant. If lost, compasses are only seven dollars at counter 108. After nine p.m. night navigation sextants are only $57.50."

The virtues of homemade bread loom larger everyday. I couldn't wait to get back from this business trip and fill the hopper of my Country Living grain mill with whole wheat berries and get back to a primal knead with real live food.

Keep the Home Fires Burning

I find nothing but pleasure in a blazing log fire sending its warmth through the living room and kitchen. I'll bet I've heard it said a hundred times by wood stove owners, "Boy, there is nothing like heat from a wood stove."

Well, I don't know whether that is true in a technical sense, but when it comes to emotional highs I dare anyone to argue the point. What could be more romantic than seeing the orange and golden flames languidly rising from logs of alder or cherry or whatever good-burning wood you can find. Then there is the gentle hiss of air being sucked in to ignite the heat-charged wood, and of course the occasional pop and zing of trapped pitch or water that punctuates the warm air.

Nobody can tell me that on a cold and windy day coming in to stand over an electric baseboard heater or a floor vent comes within a million miles of the pleasure of rubbing your hands over a well-stocked wood stove that has hot chocolate or an iron pot of stew simmering on the corner.

I like to pour whole-wheat pancake batter right on top of our wood stove and cook whopper flapjacks. I saw a sensible plaque in a friend's cabin. It said, "He who cuts his own wood is warmed by it twice." A marvelous maxim, especially on chilly days, and since I have found a monster maul with an unbreakable handle and a blade that doesn't bind, the routine goes a lot smoother. What a lovely way to keep the home fires burning—with wood, a truly renewable resource.

Contemplation

As I contemplated the early November day, the whole canvas of everything I saw seemed brushed from a palette of gray: the dark rain-filled sky, the wind-swept water and trees, and perhaps the grayest of all, the headlines of the morning news.

When both the meteorological and socio-economic climates are gloomy, it doesn't take any great insight to figure out which of the seven dwarfs I'll end up feeling like before the day is over. Fortunately, even though the front page was mongering war as inevitable, I looked up from the newspaper and saw something sitting right in the middle of our kitchen table that saved me from the grump dump. It was a Chrysler Imperial. No, not the Chrysler with white walls and leather seats—my imperial was a rose, a solid white rose with clean graceful lines. I easily imagined why they had named it *Imperial*.

I had rescued it and a fragrant pink rose with the evocative name of "Sweet Surrender" from a cold-driving rain just two days before. When I brought them in they were sheathed in damp and cold-browned outer petals. I carefully peeled off the offending rot to reveal the beauty beneath.

Now, two days later, in the warmth of the house the buds had started to open. They were beautiful. The scent from the full-flowered delicate pink Sweet Surrender was marvelous. It wafted deliciously past my nose. I pulled the vase of roses close, buried my face in the bouquet and breathed deeply of the heady fragrance. The portals of warmth and hope opened and the light chased away the gray, at least for another day.

Seventy-Six Trombones…
and Other Noteworthy Sounds.

A few weeks ago I was asked to be the master of ceremonies for a community band festival. Because of the time and travel requirements I had a "No" firmly stamped on my mind. But the next thing I knew my lips said, "Yes".

I've suffered from this lip synch problem for years. You know, not saying what you really are thinking, or not really thinking about what you are saying. So I mentally kicked myself for committing to yet another project.

I was still grumbling as I arrived at the auditorium on the night of the concert. But, wow, it only took a few notes of music to roll through the hall before my foot was tapping and my spirit was soaring. As it turned out, these weren't high school bands, but adults from eighteen to sixty-eight, all dedicated musicians sacrificing and taking time because they loved every noteworthy moment.

Six bands participated, one sponsored by the giant of the airplane industry, Boeing. I didn't hear a hint of what I'd feared. No screechy clarinets, no tremulous tubas. Nothing but full big sounds with rousing percussion and pulsing precision. The compositions of Sousa, Akers, Pryor and Holst fanned a patriotic glow through the audience.

I found myself being thankful for all the school band programs across our land that have fostered the melodic motivation for the community band resurgence now taking place in America. From the small town bands of the civil war era has come a musical heritage whose sounds, I hope, will never fade from our shores.

The Most Beautiful Thing in The World

I took a little, informal poll the other day. The question wasn't very controversial and the responses won't change anybody's foreign policy or campaign strategy. But for me? The answers made my day.

I was musing one day over the many lovely things that this old world has to offer, and I was feeling frankly thankful for them all. As I pondered, my curiosity began to pique. Surely, though my thankfulness covered a broad spectrum, there were things that I had overlooked. Perhaps some other watchful and appreciative eye had perceived beauty in something I had not even considered. The question of my poll? I asked people what they thought the most beautiful thing in the world was.

I got some marvelous answers. I asked an old Idaho farmer what he thought. With no hesitation he said, "Why, a newborn white-face calf. When that calf first comes from the heifer there is no whiter white in the world. It is absolutely beautiful."

When early spring came I watched the fields for cattle—and he was right.

I asked a young mother the same question; after a moment she said, "The most beautiful thing in the world is when two people have a really good, considerate relationship." Of course, she is right too!

A broadcaster, a long time friend, replied, "Why flowers have to be the most beautiful. That's the only thing they are here for, just to bring beauty—God's gift to man."

My answer? It has to be the look on children's faces when you praise them. An inner light dances through their eyes with the joy of being accepted and loved. With so many things of beauty surrounding us you would think that sadness should be a rare commodity.

Tracer of Lost Tools

In the heyday of the radio drama there was a show called, "Mr. Keen, Tracer of Lost Persons". Of course, this old radio show is all but forgotten, but I want to tell you I could easily write the script for a sequel, except this time I would call it "Mr. Dad, Tracer of Lost Tools". There have been times that I've almost "lost it" when a child-borrowed tool has been irrevocably lost, and that minor little fact was only discovered at the moment of critical need. On several such moments of warmth I've hotly threatened that henceforth and forever all tools would be double padlocked away in a container worthy enough to withstand the battering of tanks —and seven children.

I've mellowed somewhat over the years. The mellowing was not entirely age-induced—it was primarily brought about because of an interview I had with an elderly Italian gentleman who, when asked about his childhood, revealed bitter roots. After forty-five years that man still bore vitriolic resentment against his father. Why? Because his dad never let him use or even touch his tools.

Having just replaced a shovel that my kids had lost (for the second time), I had instant sympathy for his dad's "You can't toucha my tools" stance. But I sure didn't tell my interviewee, because obviously his dad's hard-nosed attitude about his hammers and saws had left a tender, unhealed scar.

Because of that conversation I've shelved my resolve to padlock my tools in a steel vault and never let my kids touch them. So I still beg, cajole, threaten, and remind my kids that tools are to be put away after use. And as my toll of lost tools mounts, along with the price of replacement, I try to remind myself that it's all part of the price of raising children.

Do I waver in my noble thoughts? Yeah, like yesterday when I unearthed in our driveway a long-lost wrench of mine—now well rusted. Locking them in a vault suddenly appealed to me. Oh, no, not the tools—the kids who didn't put them away.

Dedicated to all the Fathers
who have Daughters with Cars!

The evening before our second daughter, Jill, was to leave on her thousand-mile trek to college, her car developed a major oil leak. Her oil spill was Exxon Valdezian in proportion—you could follow her car anywhere over land or sea by the slick she was leaving behind. She had dropped enough oil to grease down all of the duck-tail hairdos of the fifties. I fully expected to see an aging Elvis (would he still have enough hair to slick back?) skulking down our drive to zero in on the source.

When her car cooled (an almost unknown phenomenon for that poor, driven thing) I checked all of the obvious leakables. Nothing. Then I wiped everything clean under the car and Jill did the same up above (she dived into the grease and grit with a surprising zeal) so we could hopefully see the spigotal-spot. Jill added a couple of quarts of thirty-weight to her depleted oil reservoir, then I asked her to start the engine while I remained supine beneath that grimy girth of gears to watch for blossoming little oil wells. I gingerly maneuvered my gravel-ground body to try to gain the best overall vantage point.

"Okay Jill, I think I'm at the best spot for taking it all in."

Jill turned the key. The engine shuddered to life. Great globs of oil! Viscid mung descended from everywhere! I was showered with Quaker State's best. Jill had forgotten to put the oil cap back on!

As I mused over the price of fatherhood, we started all over—this time with the oil cap in place. After ten minutes of searching we finally spotted the cause of all the despair—a little hose in plain sight, connected to a vacuum pump on the rear of the generator.

Aha, no sweat, simple to change—right? Wrong! One end of

that little puppy hose went down into a deep crevasse that made it absolutely impossible for any known tool developed by mortal man to access.

I called an Isuzu mechanic and asked if there was some secret to getting it out. He thought for awhile, or at least pretended to, and said, "Well, if you take off the front tire, then remove a rubber boot that's down there...! Right! After an hour of horror-filled futility I knew in my heart of hearts I'd never get a wrench on the end of that foul hose secreted deep in the bowels of the engine.

The final overwhelmer came when Jill moaned, "Somebody doesn't want me to go to college because I'm going to have too much fun."

I snapped back, "Well, make up your mind to study and work hard instead of just having fun so we can get this stupid car fixed." Jill then assured me that indeed she was going to give education her very all. I thought I heard a ring of conviction—for the moment at least. It was then that my wrench slipped and split the skin open on my knuckle for the second time. As I watched my blood gel I decided that maybe the dawn of a new day would bring new hope and energy in getting the impossible done. I almost believed it.

With the morning sun dawned two realities: I had more sore muscles than a Seahawk lineman and we needed some big-time help—both tool-wise and in the knowledge department. Our only hope was our mechanical-minded neighbors, the father and son duo of Dick and Bob Ellis. Between them they had tools that even Boeing hasn't dreamed of and knowledge that was heady stuff to mechanical half-wits such as myself.

Dick, Bob, and their tools arrived after supper. After some probing Bob suggested what I had feared all along, that we undo the mounts and jack up the engine to give us the leeway we needed. After using a vast array of pry and crow-bars we finally had enough slack space to unscrew that hummer of a hose all the way out. Then, to cheers all around (we had a crowd of about eight by then) I held up that little six-inch hose as proudly as though we had just delivered a baby.

Bob muttered something about Hirohito's revenge as he wiped the grease from his hands and arms. Then he said, "I was really impressed by how Jill got right in there and helped no matter how grimy and hard the job."

Then as he started to walk away he smiled. "But I'm real happy at the thought that this car is going to be out of the state by tomorrow."

I, too, felt a surge of joy at the very thought.

Lunch Break

It was a beautiful October day. The mercury rose to new heights and gently nudged its silvery nose against the seventy-degree mark on our porch thermometer. It also nudged my desire-not-to-work.

To me, being inside on a sublimely sunny day is worse than being trapped in an ice cream factory with my mouth taped shut. But calls had to be made and a script finished, so I set lunch as the time to escape to the sunscape. But my longing kept pulling; the lake was as smooth as glass and noon seemed a world away.

But noon did come and I grabbed the kayak paddle off the porch and walked through the cool grass to the lake. The orchard still harbored a few apples and I plucked one that had rose-red cheeks and pushed it deep into my pocket as a hedge against future hunger on my paddle around the lake.

By the time I slid the kayak into the water a little breeze had spanked the surface into bathroom-window white. A distant neighbor had launched his mega-horse speedboat into the lake. He was vrooming out billows of exhaust and cutting an ugly gash into the once calm lake.

I was thankful that the water healed quickly and wished with all my might he'd be still. Our wills must have been one, for he cut the engine, put his feet up and drifted on the breeze. I greeted him as I paddled by. He said he wished his lunch break would last forever; I wished the same. Of course, it didn't but its memory will touch my forevers with its golden glow.

I'm sometimes dismayed at how long it takes we humans to learn things—even simple things like when to pick an apple. Years ago a nursery man and I were driving out the January chill as we stood gratefully around his oil burner when he suddenly said, "Jack, I've got something I want you to taste."

He handed me an apple from a box and I took a big bite and marveled at how crisp and juicy it was.

"Must have had this in cold storage to keep it so firm?" I guessed.

"Nope," he replied. "My Melrose apples have been in this room ever since I picked 'em last fall."

Well, I was the Adam to his Eve-like offer, and I bought two trees, pruned, fertilized and waited; six years later both trees had produced a cumulative total of eight apples. But this year, this year, there was a bumper crop. The branches were bowed with their burden. I was so excited about the bounty I could hardly wait for the harvest. By the middle of September I couldn't contain myself, so I got some boxes to contain the apples. I was disappointed; they didn't seem as sweet and crisp as I'd remembered. They withered quickly and I wondered why.

About a month later I noticed several apples on the tree that I had missed. They were still firm and certainly rosier. I picked one and took a bite. It cracked open with a snap and the sweet tart apple juices ran down my chin. It was the Melrose that I'd remembered. My impatience had robbed the others of lasting sweet firmness. A whole bin of apples were pithy and with no savor because they had been plucked in the midst of their youth.

The Cake Covenant

Years ago, our then four-year-old looked out the window on a snowy morning and declared, "Look! Heavenly Father's put frosting on his cake." And somehow, even though many years have gone, that image still comes to mind when I see a shimmer of frost or a blanket of snow.

True, living on the earth is not always a piece of cake, but somehow that brief vision through the eyes of a four-year-old prompted me to promise that I would try to listen and look with a little more care and a little more wonder. Betimes, I really think it has helped.

One chilly evening my youngest daughters begged me to go out in the boat with them, even though the rim of the lake was sheeted with ice. I immediately stated a half dozen reasons why we couldn't go—not being able to paddle on frozen water being my strongest objection. Then I remembered my cake covenant and said, "Okay troops, get your coats, hats, and life jackets— we're going out into the arctic blast."

The ice was over an inch thick in spots, but we hacked and shoved and pushed that old canoe inch by frozen inch through that crystal barrier. For a moment I imagined that I was George Washington going across the ice-gorged Potomac. Then the ice began to thin and the boat started to glide through the more fragile stuff. We paused to watch the flags of breath unfurl from our frozen lips, and as we did we heard delicate wind chimes tinkle from the stern. I turned and saw the eddies from the boat braid the crystal shards of ice together. We sat spellbound and listened to the ethereal music of water playing against the shell of its former self—lovely frosting on His cake.

Getting Misty

When the cold winter air moves over the warmer land and river, it magically condenses the moisture into droplets of fog. The ethereal scenes it creates sometimes mystify me.

It seems that fog has plagued much of the nation at one time or another, and just hearing the mention of heavy fog suddenly conjures up memories of my Dad driving our 1945 Plymouth through fog so thick that he had to stick his head out the window while we crept along at ten miles per hour.

Fog can be miserable and frightening to drive or fly in, but it can also imbue its own brand of beauty and peace. I don't think anything is more breathtaking than to look down on a valley that is blanketed with fog and see small islands of treetops thrusting up from the woolly gray that stockings their feet. I'd never known those spots were loftier than the rest—until the fog had quietly snuffed from vision the baser stuff and left the highlights for hill dwellers and birds to see.

Late one winter afternoon I climbed up to a plateau above the damping gray. I looked across the fog-swathed valley to the mountains on the east. The sight of the sun and snow-glazed peaks was almost painful against the dusky sky and the endless valley of gray beneath. The mountains' majesty was a hundred times enhanced because no busy valley could be seen. Its beauty overwhelmed. Funny, even when I'm above the fog, my vision can still get a little misty.

The Case of the Summertime Santa Claws

This spring we found ourselves with two young, pregnant cats. Our younger children were ecstatic with anticipation. They prepared a box with a clean, fluffy cloth for the mothers and off-spring to be. One morning we all noticed that their tummies were trimmer and that the blessed event had occurred. But, of course, not in the place we humans had hoped for. The children searched the woods and tried tracking those tricksters through thorn and thicket. Nothing.

On several occasions we noticed the cats in the house, but everyone denied letting them in. One day I noticed Chex, one of the cats, clamber up the Cascara tree next to our house and disappear up onto the roof. Then Joel reported some scritching sounds in the ceiling of his basement bedroom. It was too bizarre to be true, but I checked anyway. I peered up our downstairs fireplace chimney. Sure enough, there were scratch marks in the soot of the chimney liner—followed by tiny, sooty paw-prints that led to an open rafter space above the bedroom.

Those implausible pussy cats were going to the roof, climbing the chimney, and extending their claws so they could scratch-slide their way to the bottom. All this so they could have their little bundles of joy in our basement.

Hmmm! I wonder if they might have gotten the idea when they last heard me read *The Night before Christmas* to the kids the previous winter. Do you suppose that those cats thought that Claus was spelled with a "w"?

The Missing "Million Dollars"

What has one eye, one-and-a-half ears, a raggedy arm pit, and is worth at least a million dollars? Any parent who has hung around long enough to bear the title of parent probably recognized, at least in vague generalities, the million-dollar item that I described. And if you parents don't recognize this most priceless of objects, then certainly your young children will—for what child hasn't had a doll, fuzzy toy, or teddy bear that has been companion, confidant, comforter, and cozy consort. And no matter how tattered or torn, mauled, or mangled, when misplaced or lost, which parent wouldn't give a million to have it back?

Without it the child becomes a wailing, woebegone wretch. Sleep doesn't come to either child or parent. Food won't be eaten. The child becomes a clinging, sniveling, impossible little twerp.

It is then that an intuitive con artist could ask for a million bucks in return for the teddy, and the beleaguered parents would gladly hawk their soul to get 'ol teddy back just so some semblance of peace and normality would return.

Just last week my four-year-old lost her "Lemmy" bear. Life became unbearable. Our daughter could no longer sleep in her own bed because she was scared without Lemmy. She moped, she swooned; we even prayed for Lemmy's return. Boy, did we pray.

Miraculously, our daughter's big brother found Lemmy a day later under a board outside. There was rejoicing. The smudged Lemmy was kissed and hugged. Was I grateful to see Lemmy again? Well, at this very moment, I have a tattered, soft, little yellow bear sitting on my lap helping me type this piece.

Lemmy's proud four-year-old owner is by my side with beaming face and dancing eyes, nodding approval for every letter that Lemmy types with his soft little paw held in mine.

Yep, its nice to have 'ol Lemmy back!

Cat Choreography with a Crumb

A neighbor was complaining that too much of her life was spent in the food business—preparing it and serving it, not to mention the clearing and cleaning.

Here's some food for thought: Just about everybody likes it, some people adulate it, but for those whose lot it falls to prepare and serve it, the seemingly incessant demand for food often weighs heavy (and that's not just on the bathroom scale).

Spouses and children want food on time, and some, all the time in between time. If you have pets you really perpetuate the food-factory syndrome. My neighbor bemoaned that without thinking she had added to her constant catering woes by training her parrot to ask for a cracker. Thousands of crackers later *she's* going a little crackers. It was all pretty discouraging.

After she left I opened the fridge door to see what comfort I could find. There was nothing readily munchable except an old peanut butter sandwich that my kindergartner had B and A'd (bit and abandoned).

As I clutched the sandwich I noticed through the patio door our four cats staring at me iron-eyed. (Iron-eyed isn't quite as menacing as a steely stare). Their unblinking gaze bored into me. I took a step, their heads swiveled as one. I tore off a bit of bread and walked toward the glass slider. They rose in unison on their hind legs and did a purrfect pussy cat pirouette. I pushed open the door and suddenly there was a cauldron of cats as they boiled into the house. Cat choreography with nothing but a crumb. Gads, the power of food is awesome!

Five Yellow Stripes

"Summertime, and the livin' is easy"—unless something is bugging you. If anything can bug me about summer, it's bugs. Oh, a leaf-lopper lunching on my lettuce is livable, as long as he leafs some for me. But this summer numberless hordes are advancing like hungry Huns- stripping bare all that is near, dear, and green.

Well, it's the tent caterpillars that are making me tense. I've sprayed repeatedly with stuff that supposedly puts the jinx on caterpillars' digestive tracts, but not on bees and man. I believed the label. Ha!

We arrived home after a week's vacation only to find furry skeletons where trees once stood. Our raspberry plants were a mass of squiggling orange fuzz. A neighbor's apple trees were tented in cocoons of death. There was not even a glimmer of green anywhere to be seen in the smothering masks that enshrouded those poor naked Gravensteins.

It got worse! As the week waned a veritable carpet of caterpillars inched its way across roads and houses. Our mail carrier refused to open a mailbox covered with living mange. Our road had five yellow stripes. Four of them would squish and ooze if you stepped on them. If you walked under anything your hair and clothes would be anointed with both caterpillars and their droppings. Gross and gloom!

But, just as my neighbor was ready to lay the ax to his stripped apple tree, an old-timer said, "Wouldn't do that. Thirteen years ago we had caterpillars worse. My wife begged me not to chop our cherries. Golly, next year it had the best crop ever!"

The moral? Wear an old hat and wipe your shoes often. This too shall pass.

Strawberry Pops and More

As I was down on my knees picking strawberries with my children this summer, I started dredging up memories of my strawberry days as a kid. I easily remembered the sore, bruised knees from kneeling on hard clods of dirt and stones all day. I remembered walking like an early version of R2-D2 because my jeans were plastered stiff with a vexing mixture of mashed strawberries and mud.

The memories verged on sweetness as I recalled finding those occasional gigantic ripe-to-perfection berries that kept whispering, "Eat me, Eat me". I don't know how many kids could refuse a talking berry, but I sure couldn't. So I'd pop that delicious prize in my mouth and let those marvelous juices bathe my throat with sweet strawberry goodness.

Then there was Lisa Gionelli, the cute little Italian girl who could pick two flats of berries for every one of mine—probably because I was busy watching her instead of picking. The boys used to make snide remarks about her because we were jealous of her speed, but secretly most of us had a crush on her.

Well, despite the Beatles singing "Strawberry Fields Forever", the fields where I once picked are gone. They now have tracts of frame houses planted there. I was suddenly brought back to my present-day patch when my oldest son, who was picking next to me, said," Hey dad, do you hear the neat little popping sounds the ripe berries make when you pick them off the vines?"

I hadn't, but he was right. The berries that were ripe to perfection, but still firm, popped with a clean sharp crack—like champagne corks. Maybe the berries were celebrating their release from the vines. With some practice I got so I could pull a bunch of berries at a time, releasing a cannonade of celebrating strawberries. How could I have missed that as a kid? Too bad, but some how I did.

How to Survive a Teenage Daughter

Can a doctorate in psychology or Logic 405 really help in surviving your children's teen years? I doubt it. Besides, the psychologists who were in vogue while I was going to college are now as out-of-style as sunbonnets at the Ritz. Nope, the only way that you are going to survive the teen-age years of your children is to take careful notes and be a humble learner while you're attending the twelve-year college called adolescence.

I'm sure God designed it so parents would have twelve whole years of preparation and intensive hands-on instruction, so to speak, before we are allowed to referee on the chaotic battlefield of teendom. The following incident proves my point:

One very drippy morning my fourteen-year-old daughter informed me that she had missed the bus, the implication being, of course, that I run out to the car and drive her the seven miles to school. I had indul-gently done just that on more than a few occasions, but this morning was different. Our old van had gotten tired and the steering wheel no longer steered.

"I'm sorry," I said. "I just haven't got a way to get you to school. You should have been ready on time."

That brought tears and an outburst, "But I've just got to be there. I'm in a play…they're all depending on me…I'll get an 'F' if I'm not there!" There were more sobs and more of, "I'll just die if I don't get there."

Being a softy, and priding myself on thinking well in an emergency, I called a friend. Yes, she would pick up my daughter. I triumphantly told my daughter of my saving efforts. Was I greeted with smiles and hugs of thanksgiving?

Nope! Another outburst of tears. "But Daddy, that's so embarrassing having to be picked up. What if she doesn't have time to do it? Her day is ruined. How humiliating!"

I made her go wait in the rain—while I took copious notes.

Say Goodbye to Childhood

Goodbyes can be easy or tough. Of course, a lot depends on who you are saying goodbye to.

When you live with someone for eighteen years you should know that person well. That includes their strengths and the weaknesses through the good times and the not-so-good. So when it comes time to say goodbye to a son or daughter, even though you know the inevitable has come, and that millions of children prior to yours have survived the cut and made marvelously grand and responsible adults, you still find yourself praying fervently that they will be humble and understanding students as they confront the lessons of life.

Some nine-hundred miles from home we tearfully dropped our daughter Amy off at her college dorm. On our trip home I asked Ann, my wife, to record a few of her thoughts.

She wrote: "This past year Amy has been anxious to be on her own. She and her sister Jill shared a room and would often have long talks late into the night, but just as often they would be arguing over bedroom priorities. Jill was anxious to have the room to herself. The time had come, for Amy's best interest and growth, for her to leave. We were looking forward to a little more harmony, life slightly less hectic and confusing because of one less person to account for and schedule around. I had no idea how hard it would hit me when the time actually came to say goodbye and give the last kiss and hug.

Even now, as I write this three days later, I want to cry. A vital part of me has left—an attachment of eighteen years is no longer there; not just someone I loved and understood, but someone who had come to love and understand me, my good friend, is gone."

P.S. *Gone* has an air of finality; it sounds pretty terminal.

Well in this case *gone* was pretty short lived. Amy, her husband and new born daughter lived with us for eighteen months while her husband finished school. Now they live a mere twenty-minute drive away. Good blessings all around.

Fish Story

I'm always a sucker for a good animal story, but when you can combine an animal story with a fish story, you've got an awesome thing.

I haven't met a lot of cats that I felt were truly memorable. But I don't think I could ever forget Blackie. I met Blackie when I was ten. I don't remember playing with her, or even petting her. Of course, she wasn't mine. She belonged to my Aunt Florence. At least my aunt thought the cat belonged to her, but I'm almost sure that in Blackie's independent, feline mind she didn't belong to anyone, and, considering her unusual characteristics, maybe not even to the cat family.

My Aunt Florence lived on the same little lake that I did. Then, but not now, it was full of such marvelous things as cut-throat, perch, turtles, and some ugly, but delicious, catfish. I don't think Blackie had a particular penchant for catfish. I suspect that she liked all fish, but the catfish were just easier to catch. And that is just what Blackie would do—catch the fish—all by herself. No help!

The catfish's habit of laying their eggs in shallow, sunny water aided Blackie immensely. The newly-hatched catfish swam in a squiggly little ball while the parent catfish would hover close by. That's when Blackie would move into action. I'd watch her pussyfoot onto a dock or log, then wait patiently until the big catfish swam close. Then whip! Splash! Blackie would be on top of the finny critter's back until she wrestled it to shore! I suspect I'll never see another cat fish for catfish, but the Blackie of my youth did! Honest!

Haunting Fire Trail

How do you make somebody who thinks they are nobody feel like somebody again?

Nobody has ever said that being a teenager is easy, and I'm convinced it's tougher than it has ever been. I remember well my youngest son's fourteenth summer. He'd spent a couple of frustrating days trying in vain to get together with some friends. Zero results reduced him to moaning that nobody liked him. Life was no fun, he'd never be popular, etc, etc.

He was also feeling the absence of his older brother, who had left some six months earlier. Besides wrestling with him, my oldest son and his friends would occasionally invite Jason to go with them in their gleeful efforts to perpetuate a local myth. The gist of the story is that the ghost of a vengeful Indian would appear on moon-full nights and angrily wave his lantern on Fire Trail Road.

Well, my oldest son and his friends were more than happy to attract additional myths to the flame of gossip by dressing in tattered clothes and waving an old lantern in the center of the road. To the absolute delight of my youngest son, he was invited by the older boys to tag along on several occasions. All that ended when the older group went their separate ways.

Well, it happened that when Jason's cup of self-esteem was empty, it was also a full moon night. Just before ten there was a knock at the door. I heard a voice ask, "Is Jason there?" I was miffed at the lateness, then realized it was my oldest son's friends and welcomed them. They wanted Jason to join them. My fourteen-year-old beamed.

I said, "Yes," and Jason floated out of the house and through the woods on a sea of self-esteem. Some thoughtful older boys had filled his sail full.

Jimmy the Eagle

This is the story of a young Boy Scout who actually flew, but not with the artifice of wings or props or jet packs. No, this twelve-year-old flew unencumbered, as free as a swallow in May.

Young Jimmy Rankel's flight was pure spontaneity. No drum rolls, no anticipatory hush held the crowd like mush. No, you see, the scout camp was equipped with two tall telephone poles with an industrial-strength bungie cord strung between. A veritable sling shot for humans—with a seat belt in the middle.

Jimmy Rankel was scared spitless. Jimmy just knew he'd lose his lunch in front of all the scouts. His disgrace would be total. But to be "chicken" and say "No" to the bungie ride would be worse still.

His fear mounted almost to hysteria as they held the seat for him to get in. They buckled his safety belt. Then ten pairs of strong arms steadily pulled him back. His fingers were a frenzied flurry as he wrenched at the seat buckle. He had almost freed himself when the count hit three.

Twang! He shot forward like a bullet toward the sky. But Jimmy didn't stop when the cord's power was spent. No, not on Jimmy's life, he and the bungie seat parted ways and Jimmy kept going skyward. The ground-bound scouts stared goggle-eyed as they witnessed Jimmy's heavenward projection. He soared over the aspens—he spread his arms and thrust his chin out, feeling the wind beneath his wings, and in a graceful arc he swooped toward the trees.

The awed scouts were galvanized into action and they roared like an engine into the grove to find the now spent bullet of a Tenderfoot. When they found Jimmy he was standing, scratched, shirt torn—and smiling. They let out a mighty cheer and hoisted him to their shoulders.

Nobody remembered the fearful, timid Jimmy who had declined the bungie seat the day before. All they saw was Jimmy the eagle, Jimmy the fearless, Jimmy the boy-who-had-flown.

Saying Goodbye to the Winter—with Guns

The morning fog lingered, then hardened on frozen branches, and left a talcum dusting on all the trees and shrubs. It was a little after seven as I walked down from the woodpile with some split logs in my arms. When I heard the ear-rending racket I forced my eyes upward to scan our cold and leafless maple tree, and there a pair of Douglas squirrels were perched, trading a cacophony of chirps and squeals.

I stood and watched and listened and, if I hadn't known better, I would have sworn that those chirpy little fuzz balls were miniature mechanized toys. It almost seemed as if their chirps were so powerful that the squirrels were propelled (or should I say jerked) forward by the very force of the chirp—like a sneeze can rock some people back on their heels.

There they were, chirp-jerking forward an inch at a time with their tails twitching in robot-like unison. I humored myself by carefully scanning their backsides to see if there were really a wind-up key going round or maybe a slot for a battery pack. Then the most aggressive of the two increased his speed, both of his chirp and jerk, about twenty-fold. The sound became a machine-gun staccato, and instead of inch gains up the tree trunk, the squirrel bounded by feet and yards toward what seemed to be a shy girl mate.

She turned and leaped. Who wouldn't with a hairy machine gun coming toward you? A hot pursuit began through branch and thicket. The mechanization was gone. They were suddenly real-life, intelligent little spirits, thoroughly enjoying a pre-spring gambol on a frosty March morning.

The Celestial Light Show

One of my favorite pastimes is lying on our old dock on a clear summer night with some of my children and watching the scroll of heaven unfold. The most delicious part is waiting for the unexpected to happen. We are seldom disappointed.

When my kids and I go out on a summer night to star gaze, we take blankets to throw over the old, rude planks of the dock so we can gaze divinely supine at all the heavens have to offer. Around the end of July the show gets really exciting—sometimes fast and furious. The two midnight summer showers of shooting stars that bring the most oohs and ahs are called the Delta Aquarids and the Perseids. The night to watch for the Delta Aquarids shower of meteors is during the last week of July.

Some star watchers say they see over twenty shooting stars an hour during the Delta showers. For really fast-paced gazing, almost like watching a tennis match, the Perseids shower, August eleventh through the thirteenth, can't be beat. From fifty to seventy-five glowing meteors an hour will delight your heaven-gazing eyes. Unfortunately, the Perseids shower may lose a little luster some years because the moon is too big and bright. The best star-studded show may be the Delta Aquarids.

But either cosmic shower will provide a lovely time to communicate with your children about heavenly things.

The Ice Cream Equation

Ice cream-aholics will certainly lend a sympathetic ear to my creamy and caloric confessions. Ann and I are rather strong-willed when it comes to really good ice cream. We're strongly in favor of it. We don't dawdle even a second on caloric guilt trips. Why, two or three times a month we fill our old White Mountain ice cream maker with cream from the farm and start cranking.

We justify this delicious splurging by roundly rationalizing that if we hand crank we will burn off the creamy cold calories that we are about to ingest. "No crankie—no cream" is our motto.

Aside from the homemade ice cream, Ann and I have found that there is one of the so-called gourmet ice cream bars that truly deserves the attention of ice-creamaholics (and chocoholics) everywhere. It has smooth, rich, chocolate ice cream inside. Ah, then that little beauty is dipped in dark Belgian chocolate. Ho, ho does that do sinful things to your taste buds.

We bring those bars home in a plain brown wrapper so the kids won't see them. We put them in the freezer in a package marked "chicken liver". The kids wouldn't dare lay a finger on that package even after a three-day fast.

After bedtime I sneak the "chicken-liver" package into our bedroom and we languidly luxuriate in creamy chocolate bars with the dark chocolate coats. On Haagen Daaz nights our goodnight kiss may be bittersweet but it seems to linger longer.

The Cedar Slip-Stream

To me, driving the freeway during rush hour has all the appeal of getting a rabies shot from an Army trainee. Ughh! In short, I'd rather not! But like most Americans, I find myself plying those ribbons of concrete, praying that I'll be spared the wrecking wrath of those who want to force their vehicles into space that doesn't exist, or think speed limits are the number of uppers you can pop in five minutes.

One afternoon I was caught in the Seattle freeway's four-thirty frenzy. I was station hopping on the radio, trying to find something stimulating instead of degrading or depressing, when suddenly my whole world transformed. There I was in a quiet, sylvan glade of giant Alaskan cedar!

No, I hadn't completely lost it. The aroma of rain-soaked cedar had suddenly engulfed me. I was awash in the vision of tall stately cedar trees with the frond-like boughs moving in the breeze. I shook my head. I was still on the road, but in front of me was a double tractor-trailer stacked high with freshly split cedar shakes. A rain shower had brought out its pungent best, the scent was streaming out behind and flowing through my car's vents.

My mind did the rest. As long as I stayed behind the cedar I was locked in the privacy of a pristine wilderness. If the semi switched lanes, I frantically tried to follow. If he sped up, I sped up. I hate tailgaters, but there I was sticking like cedar-sap right behind this eighteen-wheeler. It wasn't until I saw the flashing red lights that I came back to the freeway of life.

Incidentally, have you ever tried to explain to the State Patrol that the reason you were speeding and tailgating is because you were lost in the woods?

The Piano

Bonnie Davis had dreamed, for as long as she could remember, about having her own piano, but circumstance and finances had made it impossible. Then one day a friend at church offered Bonnie a piano.

"How much do you want for it?" She asked.

"Why, nothing, nothing at all. It's free."

Bonnie thrilled at the prospect of possessing her own piano. It was an old upright Fisher, manufactured in 1889, and built as solid as the proverbial brick outhouse, but ten times heavier. She called on some friends to help move it. I happened to be one of them.

Six of us groaned and strained to heft that hunk of brass and wood up ten steep and narrow basement stairs. As we panted and inched upward I had a foreboding that someone would slip or lose a grip. I was on the bottom end of the ton-o-tunes, so I felt that paranoia was my prerogative, especially since I would be the recipient of not only the Fisher, but also my fellow piano-packing compatriots. By the tenth step we were all wheezing like the bellows of an old pump organ—ah, but I mix my metaphorical instruments. When we finally eased it into the bed of the small pickup I said a prayer of thanks. I would have done well to add a postscript and request the gift of wisdom.

The tires bulged—there was some concern. Like a faint and familiar melody the suggestion of using securing-ropes to steady the top-heavy old girl floated by, but the heavy beat of "Macho, Macho Man" seemed to drown out the refrain of restraint. Reassuring comments were tossed around: "Don't worry, we'll drive real slow." And "The four of us will ride in the back with the piano—we'll hold it steady no matter what."

Bonnie, her husband and I drove behind the precious piano.

Things went well until—until we rounded the curve by the fire station. The heavy piano began to tip. Then in excruciatingly slow motion it lost to the tug of gravity, swung over the bed of the pickup and smashed against the road bed. Bonnie's dreams lay scattered on the ground. The piano keys were strewn on the blacktop as if a free-for-all slugfest at a dental convention had been held on that very spot.

As we gathered around and stared at the remains, the silence was so profound it would have muted a rock concert. Bonnie's cheeks glistened with tears. We quietly gathered up piano keys and carefully lifted the wounded Fisher back into the truck.

Several weeks after the accident I garnered the nerve to drop by Bonnie's house. As I walked to the door I heard music—piano music. The old Fisher was standing only a little less majestic than before. Bonnie, her husband and friends had painstakingly bent and fitted and glued. Bonnie had paid with the labor of love. Bonnie's old upright Fisher had become a grand.

What's Mine is Yours...If You Really Want It.

I remember well a day some years back. I was late for an appointment, and to my chagrin I couldn't find my hair brush. In my dash I glanced into the bathroom and saw our one-year-old happily sloshing in the toilet bowl.

With a stern "No, No" stamped on my visage and my voice I charged into the bathroom. To my dismay, clasped in her little sloshing hand was my hair brush. I knew toilet water was fashionable in some circles, but this was going too far.

I extracted her from the bathroom, held the brush gingerly between my thumb and forefinger, saw my watch registering the lateness of the hour, shrugged and muttered, "What the heck...."

I gave the brush several quick rinses under the faucet, then gave my hair the necessary swipes and thought to myself, "I'll give this brush a thorough washing when I get home tonight." I thought no more about the ill-fated brush that day.

In fact, it wasn't until I arrived home that evening that I saw Jason, my very persnickety ten-year-old, vigorously brushing his hair with my brush. "I can never find my brush, Dad. I've looked all over," he moaned.

My suspicion is that his "brush-looking" time measured less than a nanosecond. The temptation to tell him the hair brush story, with a few slightly indelicate embellishments, loomed large. It would be a bit of a hoot to see him (as the teen vernacular would put it) gross out.

After some deliberation I felt a "Super Bowl" scenario was not the way to go. Not because it wouldn't be fun to watch his expression, but because, after all, it had been a long day and the peace and quiet seemed a more attractive choice.

The Summer Job

I'd fight to the death for the principle of free enterprise. But when your children practice it, look out! It may be the death of you!

My thirteen-year-old son was moping about because he didn't have a summer job. I suggested taking some small flyers around the neighborhood and soliciting lawn-mowing jobs. Somehow the flyers never made it off the ground, so to speak. Boy, do I thank heaven for that!

But through word of mouth and some telephone calls, my son came up with five lawns to mow. Three of them were spelled with a capital L, L standing for large and lumber-like (because they hadn't been cared for for so long)—in short, mini primeval forests. One of his lawns had enough nooks, valleys and cliffs to challenge even Jim Whitaker and his Sherpas.

The first lesson I learned was that lawn mowers break down or won't start for any number of reasons, most of them unfathomable to us common folk. To protect my sanity and my wallet from a continuous flow of repair bills, I enrolled my son and I in a small engines repair class. Exit fifty dollars.

Next I had to purchase thirty dollars worth of tools that were the keys to unlocking the secrets of the tricky Tecumsa or a bogged-down Briggs and Stratton. Then there were gaskets and spark plugs and mufflers to buy. My investment in my child's venture into free enterprise? Over one hundred and fifty dollars plus a second lawn mower!

Then there were the days I spent running from lawn to lawn cheering him on, filling gas tanks, doing the tough hills. I find it easy to loathe lawns. And the people who invented them—I suspect the English landed gentry were the culprits—they have cast a blight on the sanity of humanity forever. Tell me, where is the logic in weeding, feeding and watering something just so you can cut it down once a week? But to keep things in proper perspective, I have to keep reminding myself that it wasn't really grass I was raising, it was a son! He turned out just fine—a cut above the average I would guess.

The Day They Gave the Park Away

Last year the county bought a saltwater park on Port Susan, a deepwater bay on Puget Sound. It is a lovely spot, but when it was privately owned we couldn't afford the entrance fee.

Now the painted green sign said "County Park". It looked inviting, so I cranked our old car toward the entrance.

On the cliff to the right were some giant trees of the past—firs that would take at least three pairs of arms to encompass. To the left we saw a curve of beach strewn with sun-and-sea-washed driftwood. The children immediately envisioned fortresses, castles, hideouts, and jungle gyms. When the car stopped, both doors flew open as one, and we raced over the logs, jumped into sand, picked up loose pebbles, and cupped our hands to make leaky buckets. All the while we laughed and thanked God for His goodness.

We went to the park many times after that, and found others enjoying it, too. The leaves changed from green to a blaze of gold, brown, and orange. School, chill breezes, and football interfered; fewer people went. But we kept going.

Last week five-year-old Amy prepared our family home evening—a lesson, a story, and some games. She proposed we have it at the park. The vote "for" was unanimous.

Monday came; so did the clouds. Monday evening arrived; so did the rain. I vacillated, then said, "Come on, let's go anyway." My wife, Ann, hesitated, knew she was outnumbered, and headed for the closet to get the coats.

The rain had settled the dust on the gravel road between the park and home, and a clean, damp smell rose in its place. As our little car jounced over the washboard road, we sang, "Give, Said the Little Stream" because it had a verse about rain in it. The tune wandered at times, Jill was half a verse behind, and squeals from the baby punctuated here and there, but sing we did while the one remaining windshield wiper beat time. We were finishing "Oh Beautiful for Spacious Skies" (there was a small disagreement between Joel and Amy over whether that song could be sung on a rainy day) as we drove into the park entrance. One sweeping glance revealed something missing: not one car, truck or camper was there. The whole panorama was ours, unfettered and free.

Our balding tires squeegeed on the wet blacktop and we rolled to the beach and ran for the sheltered picnic table. One by one we found a place and waited to see what Amy had prepared for home evening.

Amy loved her role of conducting, and with solemnity and an air of importance she called on someone to give the prayer. She led the opening song while I dashed after Jason, who had toddled toward the incoming tide during the prayer.

Ann's treats were gobbled up faster than you can spell disaster. Then, while she held the baby (who was getting fussy by now), the rest of us played hide-and-seek in the dusk.

My lungs hurt from hard running as I wove in and out of the trees lining the beach drive. I found a trunk with a girth that exceeded mine and pressed myself close to hide from my pursuers. The rough-channeled bark gave off an aroma of wet moss and nutty autumn, and I relaxed to capture this moment as I tried to still my errant breathing lest the "enemy" should hear. It was then the thought came firmly to my mind:

"The family is a divine unit; family home evening has been given you for your joy and your salvation." The thought burned through me. I knew it was true.

"We see you, Daddy," the children squealed in delight. I let out my best lion's roar, and their shrieks filled the empty park. I bent down to catch a girl under each arm, while Joel scrambled on my back. With a full heart I hobbled back under my delightsome burden.

As we scrambled into the car and started chugging up the

hill, Joel turned and waved, "Goodbye, Park!" We all looked back. The breeze-tossed branches returned the wave.

The Dog Who Tried to Teach Us Manners

Max came to us a gift—a gift that I was sure I didn't want. The children, of course, were overwhelmingly, beggingly, beseechingly, foursquare for keeping the mutt.

The children had found him on the road, barely more than a pup, very thin, with raw and bleeding feet. I concurred that we should care for his ravaged paws and feed him "just a little".

"Don't feed him too much, " I said in my best firm and stern father's voice, "I don't want him to get used to the idea that this is his home. After all, he belongs to someone else."

We soaked his paws in warm water, cleaned them, then swabbed iodine on them. That done, we went down the road knocking on doors asking if anyone had lost a young German Shepherd/Collie mix. No one had. The children were gleeful. I was not. Adding another body, albeit a furry one, to our already large brood did not appeal to my penny and time-pinched existence. But logic, laced with a dose of sentimentality, nagged at me, and I envisioned the poor pup with raw paws travelling down mile after mile of country highways and gravely back roads to—to arrive at our door? Was it providence? Was it meant to be? I hadn't a clue. But there he was and he showed no inclination for moving on.

The children called him "Boy". Ann, my wife, and mother of all seven of the Jenkins' clan, (much experienced in naming), felt that "Boy" was not really proper enough for a dog with such a handsome visage. It was true, even I thought he had a rather noble and strong mein, and with his ears at full perk he looked dashingly irresistible. She dubbed him "Max". So "Max" it stayed, and so did he.

Not many months after Max's arrival on the Jenkins' scene we began noticing that he had a trait that separated him from all of dogdom and even from human kiddom—at least through their teenage years. He had table manners! No, we didn't let him sit at the table with us. He was strictly an outdoor dog, but Max was often beset by a politeness uncommon to both man and beast. When he was fed, even things he *really liked*, he'd merely glance into his bowl at the repast, then follow us back to the door to proffer some unspoken, but palpable, love and goodwill. Then, only after we had given a few pats and praises in return, did he go back to his meal. I comment on his "Miss Manners" attitude often in the presence of my children in the hopes that his doggy decorum will rub off on them—or at least give them "paws" for thought.

Even our neighbor, Kathy Whetstine, (our son Jason hangs around with her son), was impressed by Max's manners. While Jason and Max were visiting, Kathy gave her dog, Bosco, and Max each a doggy biscuit. Bosco inhaled the whole biscuit in a whiff! Max? Why, he gently took the biscuit in his teeth. He then looked up at Kathy and wagged his tail, walked to a grassy spot, reclined, propped the biscuit upright between his paws, then took his time licking and taking small bites, much as someone savoring an ice cream cone. He loves doggy biscuits. Kathy was virtually goggle-eyed with Max's eating etiquette, and enthused "Wow, Max is so polite. What did you do, send him to an Emily Post K-9 school? I don't think Bosco has ever tasted a thing we've fed him."

On Thanksgiving this year, Max's breeding and gentility displayed bounds so broad that they literally encompassed the very spirit of Thanksgiving.

Ann cooked the turkey giblets and neck separately for Max and the cats. I hadn't fed Max his regular ration of dog food for the day, so when I walked out of the door with a steamy-warm turkey neck, I thought Max would eagerly scarf it up as a welcome change from his dry dog food. But no, he had something else in mind. After a little coaxing, Max took the turkey neck in his mouth and I went into the house to wash my hands. I returned in just a couple of minutes and saw Max sauntering up our long driveway with the turkey neck held carefully in his teeth.

"Hey, Max, where ya going?" I yelled.

He pretended he didn't hear me and kept on going. He turned right and headed down the road. Curious, I followed up the drive, and at the top looked down the road just in time to see Max turning left into the Warsinski's place about a block away. "Ranger", Max's buddy (who visits often to steal every last morsel in Max's food bowl), lives there. I waited and watched. In a few minutes Max came out of Ranger's place wagging his tail and headed for home.

My daughter Jaime says that because I didn't actually see what happened, I can't claim this as a fact. But I would like to believe—yes, I do believe—that somehow our well-mannered Max got caught up in the spirit of Thanksgiving and took the turkey to his friend.

I went to the pantry and pulled out a box of Max's favorite "Doggy Biscuit Meaty Deluxe." I opened the porch door and called to him. When he came I held out the bone. He gently took it, laid it on the porch and came back and nuzzled my hand. I stroked his head, patted him, told him that I loved him and that

I was thankful that we had been given such a kind, gentle and grateful dog. And I meant every word.

"I Called to Say Goodbye."

Jay Menges, a long-time friend, shared this page from his journal:

Last night as I sat at my desk at work, I was provided with an unscheduled, but needed, moment of joy. I called home to see what was happening, and to remind my girls to get in bed by nine.

Katie, age twelve, answered the phone and we visited through the wires for awhile. I was filled in on the day's events, from a broken fingernail to fresh-baked cookies. Her younger sister, Mandy, was occupied elsewhere and probably dreaming of her upcoming birthday on the morrow. I said goodnight to Katie, reminding her to make sure she and her birthday sister got to bed on time.

An hour later the phone rang and a cute voice said "Hi, Daddy!" It was my youngest daughter.

"Mandy, what's wrong?"

"Nothing, I just thought I'd call you."

"Mandy, it's 9:45, why aren't you in bed?"

"I'm going to bed, I just wanted to call first and say good-bye."

"You mean goodnight, Mandy—goodnight!"

"No, " she said, "I need to say goodbye."

"Mandy, I'm not going anywhere. Are you going some-where?"

"Well, kinda…" this was followed by a giggle, "I just thought I'd call. This is the last chance you have to talk to me when I'm ten. I could feel my soul melt under the innocence of her statement. She was absolutely right.

"Yes, tomorrow you'll be eleven."

"That's right," she said, her voice filled with pride, "I'll never be ten again."

"I'm glad you called to say goodbye, Mandy. Now, you need to go to bed and get some sleep. Tomorrow will be a busy day for you."

"Okay, goodnight, Daddy."

"Goodnight, sweetheart. I love you."

"Love you, too."

That was last night. Today Mandy is eleven years old. She'll never be ten again. I'm glad she called to say goodbye.

Bittersweet Goodbye to Summer

It was the eleventh of August, and 86 degrees—as summery as summer could be. I was at peace with the world and walking hand-in-hand down a tree-lined road with my eight-year-old daughter, Leah. Suddenly, there it was! From a tree branch near the top of an old alder, a lone and yellowed leaf was fluttering down! As that leaf reached eye level it stopped its flutter, then tauntingly scribed a slow and steady arc directly in front of me. It landed with a paper-dry scritching sound right at my feet.

I tell you, it was like an icicle in my heart. I couldn't help it, that dumb leaf had evoked a dread and foreboding of something I desperately didn't want to happen—the end of summer. I resented every fiber of that dead and dried thing, and I closed my eyes and tried to wish that wretched waif back to its green and leafy bower.

It was no use. The halcyon days of warmth and melons, swimming, and children smelling of sun-kissed hair and skin would soon be gone. The robust greens from backyard gardens would soon be replaced by paler supermarket stuff trucked in from southern climes and stuffed in produce coolers. It meant the water in the lakes and ponds would soon feel the chill, and swims would be shorter, then not at all. It meant the start of eternal school buses and the breathless rush of academic activity.

When we returned from our walk I was hoping that leaf would somehow be gone—but instead there were two. Oh, those accursed appendages to a tree! Why didn't they leaf me alone— just for a little while longer!

Call Me Victoria

The Northwest November morning was squeezed full of gray—from heaven to earth and from horizon to horizon—everything was gray.

A gray-sieve of a sky was leaking steadily, forcing me to turn on time worn wiper blades that produced about the same results as a kindergartner finger-painting. Admittedly, my mood matched the weather and as I rounded the northeast corner of Lake Ki my window-smear vision revealed the water reflecting back the sky with the same pallid dullness. I longed for the sun and relief from the somber sky but my Pacific Northwest mind-fix held only the smallest ray of hope. As I steered through the last curve east of Ki I glanced at the jumble of single-wides and mobiles crowded into the small trailer park at the juncture of the McRae and Lakewood roads. I also noticed someone standing near the edge of the blacktop just a few yards outside of the park entrance.

As I squinted through the windshield I realized that it was a young woman holding a child. Standing, closely snuggled, almost hidden among the folds of the woman's long skirt, was a young girl. The woman had her arm outstretched. I thought that she was pointing at something across the road so I slowed, glanced to the other side, saw nothing, looked back at her then realized that she was hitching a ride.

My mind was closed—I don't pick up hitch-hikers, just not a prudent thing to do! I was ready to punch the accelerator to move around the curve when I heard the baby cry. I pressed the gas pedal anyway but somehow the motor seemed sluggish. The rainy tableau of mother and children was burned in my mind as I drove away, the baby's cry was nagging at me. About a block down the road I repeated the mantra, "I don't pick up hitch-hikers, I don't pick up hitch-hikers," but the echo of the baby's cry seemed to be gaining in intensity. It was then that I saw a wide driveway that was an easy pullover. I steered off the road, stopped, hesitated a moment, then offered a brief to-the-point prayer, "Lord, what do you want me to do?"

The answer was instant: The story of the Good Samaritan leaped to mind. My hitchhiker mantra faded and disappeared as I turned the car around and headed back to the corner of McRae and Lakewood.

I leaned over the seat to the passenger door and unlocked it, gave it a little shove open, muttered an apology for the scattered toys on the front seat and hastily chucked them in the general direction of the rear of our small station wagon. I then stretched to open the back door for the young girl, perhaps four or five years old. She immediately clambered in, instantly interested in the toys lying about. The mother, carrying only the child and a small bundle in her arms seemed to move with a slow and careful deliberation as she eased into the front seat next to me. She glanced briefly at me as she got in then stared straight ahead. An aura of dampness mixed with a heavy, vaguely sweet pungency clung to her. She was wearing a hip-length army surplus jacket, a long dress and what appeared to be army boots—all straight out of the Sixties. Not all that unusual since it we were barely into the Seventies.

The baby was a boy. I noticed that he looked about the same age as our youngest son Jason. My eyes were drawn to a fairly large open sore on the child's hand. I wondered if it was from a burn or a cut—I worried about him as I wondered.

Having virtually no experience in hitch-hiker repartee I muttered the inane before I asked what must be the most inevitable:

"Miserable weather, huh?"

There was a barely perceptible nod of assent. Who could deny that Northwest fact?

"Er, where are you heading?"

She shifted the position of the infant but said nothing. The rubbery squeak of my old wiper blades filled the hollow silence. I had three passengers but no destination. Why in the world had I ever stopped in the first place? My doubts started rising as the tires rolled and seconds clicked by. My mental nattering and the wiper-blades' swish almost drowned out her barely audible destination when it came.

"Seattle."

Seattle? We were about fifty-five miles north of Seattle! Well, I reasoned, I guess I can take them the five miles or so to Smokey Point, perhaps they can catch a ride from someone going south on I-5.

I glanced at the little girl playing with the toys in the back seat, then my gaze came back to the baby's hand then up to the profile of the young woman. I felt compelled to ask, though Miss Manners probably would have disapproved, "Why are you going to Seattle?"

Again silence for about four beats of the wipers then a mere whisper, " To get my children away from a bad situation."

It was the longest sentence she had spoken since our meeting, but it had a profound effect on me. Against all reason and sensibility I suddenly found myself mentally shifting my work schedule and other responsibilities to fit in taking this small family to Seattle. For some reason, for which I wasn't quite sure, it seemed important that I take this family-in-flight all the way to their destination. Little did I realize what their ultimate destination would really be.

I then realized that I didn't even know this young lady's name, nor she mine.

"My name is Jack, Jack Jenkins." My pronouncement floated for a moment then folded into a heap of unresponsive silence. I gave an expectant look toward her—still nothing! I concentrated on the shiny, rain-slick road ahead.

"Victoria, my name is Victoria." Still little more than a whisper, but progress, I thought.

"Do they call you Vicky?" I asked with hopes of making conversational inroads.

Then with surprising force and a bit of an edge to her voice, "Victoria, call me Victoria!"

In those four words she had established some dignity, an identity of worth. I made a mental note to never call her anything less than Victoria.

In my mind I worked on my schedule-juggling, came up with what seemed a workable plan and announced to Victoria, "If you wouldn't mind sticking with me while I make a few stops and complete some errands I'll take you into Seattle." For the first time since meeting she looked directly at me. There was a look of uncertainty, disbelief and other emotions that I wasn't sure that I understood.

"Do you really mean it?"

"Yes, I really mean it. I just want to call Ann, my wife, and let her know my plans and stop by the office and check to see if they have anything scheduled that I don't know about. Then we'll be on our way."

It was small, almost buried in her jacket collar, but I heard it well enough. "Thank you."

Not a lot was said, but a fair amount was communicated as we traveled south on Interstate 5. Victoria's answers to specific questions were usually vague and unspecific or simply not answered at all. I felt it was reasonable to ask Victoria her exact destination since I was the one supposedly taking her there. She finally stated that she was going to the University District. Bells went off. I had attended the University of Washington and I knew full well that many denizens of the U-District were not exactly there for higher learning. My concern grew.

Who would she stay with after she got there? She knew some people. How well? Well, er, pretty well...friends, sort of. How would she support her children? She could get a job. Who would take care of the children while she was working? Er, probably some of her friends.

It was all as vague and unsettling as the Northwest weather. My concern grew but as it grew a plan began to evolve. A plan that on the surface seemed wildly improbable, particularly when it came to meeting with acceptance or approval on Victoria's part. But the plan persisted and grew and I knew that I had to present it to this lost young woman sitting next to me despite a 99% chance of rejection.

I bolstered up my courage. "Victoria, if I could find a nice couple in the area to watch your children while you work would that be... er, okay with you?"

Again she gave me that incredulous look. Rejection was sure to follow, but like a large boulder plummeting down a mountain I couldn't stop myself, I blurted out what would surely be the final death-knell to my plan. "And would you mind if they were Mormons?"

She quickly looked away from me, stared out unseeingly at the streaming freeway traffic and slowly lowered her head. Silence!

I had blown it! I had displayed all the finesse of the proverbial *china-closet bull.*

I ventured a surreptitious look in her direction. She was nervously twisting the edge of her coat. Thinking, I imagined, that it was her bad luck to be picked up by some zealous Mormon. Still silence. Still the nervous twisting, turning of her coat. Then in a tremulous voice, (tremulous with fear I supposed) she queried, "Are you a Mormon?"

I didn't want to alarm her further, but the harm was done, I reasoned. There was only one answer:

"Yes, I'm a Mormon."

Several heartbeats passed by, then, still with eyes downcast, she uttered three words that stunned me.

"So am I."

The implications flooded over me. Now the rain and worn wipers were not the only things blurring my vision—tears were added to the mix.

As I turned off the freeway onto the 45th street exit in Seattle I hastily outlined my plan to Victoria. I cautioned that I couldn't assure its success but, that I'd do everything I could to make it happen. She nodded, still a little uncertain, then there was a glimmer of a smile. It was a wonderful smile. It swept away the Northwest gray.

There was a hamburger place a few blocks off the freeway. The hamburgers were 19 cents and local phone calls were 10 cents each (I had no idea then what a bargain they were). I ordered hamburgers and milkshakes then watched with satisfaction as my rag-tag family hungrily attacked their fast-food repast. I had enough money left over for four phone calls. I prayed I could do what I had to do for forty cents.

Fortunately, the phone book was still intact in the booth. Unfortunately, the church listings were nothing but numbers for the foyer phones and numbers that I suspected were for the Bishops' offices. The chances of getting hold of someone at 11:30 Monday morning were smaller than I could bear to think about. I was upset that we made ourselves so inaccessible. I guessed at the ward boundaries and dialed the number with foreboding. I let it ring eight times. I was just about to hang up when I heard a click—then nothing. "Hello, hello!" I shouted. Only silence was returned. I finally hung up—ten cents gone. Only three calls left!

I frantically ran down the phone list again, and there it was: *'If no answer call:'* followed by an alternate phone number. The number wasn't near the University District but it was still in the North Seattle area. I had a glimmer of hope as I dropped the second dime in the slot. The phone rang twice then an adult male voice answered.

I asked if he was a bishop and received an affirmative reply.

As briefly as I could I explained the situation.

He didn't hesitate. "I've got just the person to help you out—Bishop Earl Reed. He's our itinerate Bishop. Knowing him as well as I do, I'll just bet that he can work out something." I rejoiced—I knew Earl from the ward where I was baptized when I was 22 years old. I also knew of no one who was a more tireless worker on behalf of others. I got his number, quickly dialed and let it ring — eight, nine, ten times. The eleventh was interrupted by a breathless "Hello."

It was Earl's wife. No, Earl wasn't there but she could give me a number where he could be found. I thanked my lucky dimes, as I heard the last one clink into the receptacle. He was there. He listened, then said, "Call me back in 15 minutes and I'll see what I can put together."

"Wait!" I almost yelled in fear that he'd hang up. "If you could, I'd really appreciate it if you'd call me back. That was, well…I used my last dime when I called you."

I paced just a few yards from the phone booth wishing away any potential callers. Several people used the phone anyway so I turned my thoughts to praying they wouldn't have much to say. About twelve minutes after my initial call to Bishop Reed the phone rang, I picked it up quickly and heard the Bishops' upbeat pronouncement:

"Well, it looks like we've got a place for your mother and her children. It's only temporary, but it's a starting point while we work out something more permanent."

I thanked him profusely, announced to my trio the good news and we trundled back to the car.

Bishop Reed and the host couple were standing on the sidewalk waiting for us as we approached the house. The young couple looked slightly apprehensive. As Victoria and the children climbed out of the car the host couple's eyes got a little rounder and I saw the young husband and wife exchange a brief glance that bespoke a quorum of questions. But smiles were fixed on their faces and voices as they welcomed the small rag-tag family into their home. I let out a deep sigh of relief and thanksgiving. Thank heavens for people with faith and charity. Thank heaven, indeed!

I had promised Victoria that I would call back in a week or so to see how things were going. It was nearing the holiday season, with its usual busyness, and two weeks managed to slip by before I made the call. Bishop Reed informed me that he had found a more permanent place for our trio in a small guest-house behind a High Priest's home just a few blocks off the freeway. There was no phone in the cabin so calling wasn't an option. I asked how they were doing. He suggested that the Relief Society President in Victoria's Ward would have a good idea. She did. The children and their mother were clothed, fed, sheltered and visited. Victoria had ventured tentatively to Relief Society, but didn't stay the whole meeting.

I felt that I should return to Seattle for a visit so the next day I took some freshly baked cookies and some fruit. I found their place easily, but unfortunately didn't find them. I left the goodies with a note and promised that I would be back next week with a few small toys for the children.

I returned as promised and this time found them home. They seemed pleased to see me and the children were happy with the recycled toys that we had scrubbed and wrapped. Christmas was just a few days away. I was encouraged.

The new-year arrived and I called Victoria's host's home with hopes high.

"How are Victoria and the children doing?"

"Well, ah, we don't really know. You see, last week she and the children just left and didn't come back."

I fretted. Why did the Lord bring us together if it was going to end with no resolution? I stumbled through a list of about six whys—came up with zero answers then decided to put it in the Lord's hands. I prayed that all would be well for my little trio and,

God willing, I'd be able to help complete a job for which I somehow felt responsible.

There were no answers that I could discern. Several months dragged by and my prayers for my lost family became less frequent. I wondered if I would ever see Victoria and her children again. Then one Sunday morning during our Bishopric meeting the Bishop casually stated that he had received a phone call from a Victoria requesting some time to meet with him. My heart leapt!

"Bishop, that's the Victoria I told you about. It just has to be! Did she leave a phone number, an address?"

"No, she just said that it was important that she meet with me. We agreed to meet this coming Thursday evening at seven, she thanked me and hung up. I'll get all that information when I see her Thursday, don't worry."

I worried.

I didn't want to seem anxious. I wanted to appear self-contained, in control, a non-worrier, full of faith. I was determined not to call the Bishop—let him call me and fill me in.

Friday passed, then Saturday, Sunday arrived—still no word. I wasn't going to be the first one to bring up Victoria in the Bishopric meeting. As the meeting was drawing to a close I was ready to burst and just when my facade of patience was about to crumble the Bishop looked at me and said: "Oh, by the way, Jack your Victoria never showed up for her appointment." I was crestfallen—I was sinking and deflating in one breathless moment. Spent helium balloons had nothing on me.

He expunged what little breath I had left by adding: "Jack, I want you to find Victoria."

Me, find Victoria? Me and what army of Sherlock Holmes? The Bishop's request seemed unreasonable, I had no idea where to start. Yet, despite the seemingly overwhelming commission I had the pervasive feeling that I was the person consigned by some heavenly mandate to help bring Victoria and her children back into the fold of the Gospel. Another assignment, another responsibility—sigh! I had a growing family, a business that was struggling, and a calling in the Church that required a great deal of time. Ann and I certainly didn't need more responsibilities. I sighed again but this one held the breath of self-recrimination—I was sure God had heard all of these excuses before. I also knew that I had to cast my mental yoyoing aside and get on with the job of finding my lost threesome. But where would I look, where would I start?

I needed inspiration—what I was feeling was desperation.

I considered the idea that Victoria might have gone to a commune in the area—there were several. The problem was that communes generally didn't have phone listings—probably no phones at all. I called a friend who lived near one of the larger ones. "Actually Love Israel does have one phone. They don't always pick it up from what I hear." He rummaged around and finally came up with a number. I tried it. I let it ring seven times. Ten more and my resolve to commune with the commune flagged. The ringing stopped and I heard a muffled, "H'llo."

There was reluctance on the part of the distant male voice to discuss any of the Love Israel residences. I explained that I was following up on a call that we received—basically returning a phone call, but that…well, I really didn't know where the call came from, just who it came from. I realized that this was all sounding pretty weak, but pushed on anyway. I described Victoria and the children and held my voice and my breath.

"No, no one like that around here." Click!

Was he telling the truth or just covering? I didn't know. Maybe I would never know!

Ann's wonderful dinner after church bolstered both my spirit and my body and little Amy in her blessing of the food asked specifically for heavenly help in finding Victoria and the children. When we finished eating we had about three and a half-hours before dusk. We had little time to do the impossible. My level of faith for project Victoria had risen and I hoped it was reflected in my voice as I announced:

"Well, I'd better get in the car and start looking. I'll never find anybody sitting here at the table."

Joel, our firstborn, a tender six years of age, asked if he could go with me. I welcomed his company with the fervor of a cold man seeking a glowing fire. His enthusiasm more than made up for any dispirited views I had held during the day. Joel had gone with me to Seattle on one occasion to visit our family so he knew who they were and we had talked about them often. We put on warm coats and heavy socks (the heater in our Volkswagen Bug was a non-item). After Joel and I got in the car I ask him if he would like to say a prayer. He nodded yes, we bowed our heads and Joel asked simply and sweetly for Heavenly Father's guidance so that we could find Victoria and her children. There was no questioning, just the pure faith of a child that knew we would succeed now that we had asked God. After he said, "In Jesus name, Amen." There was a wonderful silence. No vision, no still, small voice giving direction, nothing but a palpable feeling of love for my young son and his marvelous faith.

Finally after stifling my tears I said to Joel, "Well, I know where I picked Victoria up, maybe she's moved back to where she started from. The only thing that I can think of is to go where I saw her for the first time and just start looking."

Joel nodded and smiled, " I like that idea Daddy."

His bright confirmation once again warmed me and we wasted no time in turning the car's wheels toward the intersection of Lakewood and McRae.

As we neared our fated intersection I wondered aloud. "Shall we drive up McRae and ask around? Maybe somebody knows Victoria or has seen her."

Again Joel nodded his small helmet of dark hair in sure affirmative and smiled encouragement. We turned right and headed south on McRae. As we neared the end of Lake Ki we came to a wooded road and Joel fairly shouted.

"There's a road Daddy, why don't you take that?"

"There're no houses down there, just trees as far as I can see."

Joel looked disappointed but said nothing.

We drove about a mile more on McRae and when we came to 16th Avenue NW. I turned on it and headed toward Lake Loma, a small lake that probably didn't have over twenty homes around it, most just summer cabins—so the chance of finding anyone seemed quite remote. We spattered through the mud-filled pot-holes down one driveway after another and knocked on the doors of each home. The owners were usually cordial but none were helpful in our quest. We continued full circle around the lake with the same degree of success. No one had heard of or seen anyone resembling Victoria and her children. The shades of darkness were drawing closed—we had little time left for our Victoria search. I suggested to Joel that it might be best if we headed for home and come back another time when we had more daylight on our side. I saw disappointment move like a cloud over my little boy's face, and I was suddenly filled with the poignant desire that his prayers in behalf of Victoria and her children might be answered and that his child-like faith might be reaffirmed.

I glanced at my watch, "You know, I think we just might have time to knock on a few more doors if we hurry."

Joel's face brightened.

My intent was to drive down to Lake Ki and knock on some doors around Ki, but as I sped toward my destination Joel cried out again.

"Daddy, there's *that* road!"

"What road?"

"You know. The one you said there were no houses on."

I nodded affirmation and kept driving, eager to get to the houses.

"Please Daddy let's go down that road."

I started to object, slowed the car, then stopped and backed up to the road.

"Thank you Daddy."

We had driven about half a mile and saw nothing but trees, but as we crested a hill we saw a fairly large wooden sign with bright painted flowers decorating the borders. Within those borders were printed these words, *Stoned Ridge*!

I knew without question—we had found Victoria!

The *Stoned Ridge* driveway was deeply rutted and potholed and it rattled both the aging Volkswagen and our bones as we cautiously made our way to a destination and destiny that was as yet unknown. There were several overturned junker car bodies to the right of the drive and to Joel's delight several goats were sticking their heads out of the window of one of the rusting hulks staring at us with large, unblinking, yellow eyes. A few yards further down the road stood an A frame building. The only signs of life were chickens and goats—no humans in sight. I felt a small shiver of apprehension flicker through me as I raised my hand to knock on the roughhewn door. I knocked. Nothing! I knocked again. Still no answer. We lingered for a moment at the door because I thought I heard some movement inside. I gave one more tentative rap on the door but was greeted with silence, so Joel and I turned and walked across the yard toward the driveway. Suddenly we heard a roar—a vehicle was speeding down the drive sending geysers of muddy water shooting in a hundred directions as its churning wheels pounded the brimming potholes. The shiver became a full-fledged shudder as I pulled Joel with me and lunged into the tall grass at the side of the drive. Like a screaming banshee the truck careened through the mud toward us and slewed to a stop just a yard from where we stood.

Two hirsute men, both with long beards and beyond-the-shoulder hair were in the pickup's cab. The man on the passenger side appeared to be in his late sixties, his gray hair unkempt, his eyes as glazed as frosted doughnuts—he stared straight ahead seemingly not even noticing us. The driver's eyes however drilled into us with a venomous heat. He was not happy to see us.

I told my lips to put on a pleasant, warm smile—they were working up to the task until the driver rolled down his side window and with a practiced movement pulled a rifle from the his gun rack. I lost track of my lips completely when he pointed the muzzle of his gun right at my chest and demanded, "What are you doing on my property?"

I suspect it took a moment for my lips to remember how to form the words but I managed:

"We came to visit Victoria." The knowledge that Victoria lived there was never in question. It was an absolute.

"Who in the —are you?"

"I'm Jack, Jack Jen..."

He cut me off, "Yeah, I've heard of you!"

I was a little surprised that Victoria had told him about me, but all thoughts of surprise drained when I heard the chilling sound of his rifle's safety latch being released.

Fervent prayer flooded my soul as I saw his rifle barrel move slowly up until it was aimed directly at my head. I tried to position Joel behind me without making any move that the rifleman might misinterpret—all the while asking God for the immediate favor of safety for Joel and me that we could live to be of help to Victoria and the children.

Time and tongue seemed petrified, then both thawed and I some how managed to speak with a steady voice.

"Is Victoria here now?"

He glared at me a moment, lowered the gun slightly, then surprised me by giving me an answer that seemed to carry overtones of civility.

"Victoria got some vibes that her Grandmother in California was sick so she and the kids split to go down and see her."

I actually managed a genuine and heartfelt smile.

"I hope that her Grandma is alright. I'm sure Victoria will be able to help her while she's there."

I put my arm around Joel's shoulder, we turned—all the while praying that any move we made wouldn't provoke the man with the rifle. As I took a step toward our car I spoke. "Oh, would you mind telling Victoria when she comes back that Jack and Joel came by to visit." Then I added as nonchalantly as I could. "And, would you mind asking her to give me a call when she comes back?"

His brow lowered, His eyes tightened, then in a gruff mumble he said, "Maybe, maybe not!"

We waited. Every day our family prayers included Victoria and the children. A month passed. I was beginning to fear that Victoria's hirsute husband's "…maybe *not*." was going to hold sway. I considered revisiting *Stoned Ridge,* but the well-remembered black hole aimed directly between my eyes brought a swift and leaden unleavening to that idea. Then one afternoon while I was working in the garden Joel came running out and excitedly shouted.

"Daddy, Daddy, somebody's on the phone for you. I, I think it's Victoria!"

He was right.

Several days later I met with Victoria. She had become convinced that leaving her husband and filing for a divorce was the only way she could sever the ties that bound she and the children to his abusive influence. Having met her husband I could certainly understand her desire, but I felt that I had a responsibility to meet with him and see if there was any willingness on his part to save the marriage by stopping his drug dealing and usage. I made an appointment to meet he and Victoria at their place. I tried to schedule the meeting at Church because it was safer home ground for me, but he was adamant.

"I'm not going to meet in any d____ church! If you want to talk to me you can d___ well come to my place."

I went to his place. My armor was many prayers.

When I arrived it was almost dusk. The pot-holes were still there, the overturned junkers were there, but the goats, as far as I could see, were not. I approached the A-frame with caution, knocked on the door and waited. Victoria answered the door and greeted me with a large smile. Her husband stood a few feet behind Victoria and greeted me with surly insouciance. It was virtually dark inside the house and I realized that they had no electricity when Victoria took an oil lamp, lit it and hung it from a beam. Victoria offered me a seat on a bench behind me, so I moved backward in the crowded little room and sat with my back toward the wall of the cabin. We had barely begun a strained dialogue when the lamp began to sputter, then it flickered and went out. He muttered something about being out of kerosene. Victoria apologized. I responded by saying that I didn't mind a bit and that I had had many good conversations in the dark when I was in the army and later on my mission in Korea. Victoria apologized again.

Our conversation did not go well. He was intent on haranguing me about America's use of the atomic bomb. He tried to tar me with his war-mongering-militaristic-capitalist-brush because I had submitted to the draft and served in Korea. The more he attacked me the more convinced I became that he had chosen to dodge the draft to serve his own selfish ends rather than to serve the cause of peace. Since when did destroying people's minds, souls and bodies with drugs bring peace? I tried to shift the conversation repeatedly to his role as father and husband but he knew well that that was a slippery slope for him, and every time I made the attempt he would escalate his offensive against me and America in general.

In retrospect it was a rather strange and ironic setting: Three people sitting in the deepening gloom—two praying for light, one intent on immersing us all in darkness.

During one of Victoria's husband's long tirades I felt a nudge, then a tug on my jacket near my neck. I turned quickly only to feel something, warm, damp and alive against my cheek. The *something* snorted out a hot fetid breath right in my face. I had discovered one of the missing goats. I don't know how tempered my response was, but I must of let out a surprised snort of sorts in return.

Victoria laughed, "Why that's only Dolly. She's due soon, so we've kept her inside where it's warm and dry."

Dolly had provided a merciful moment of remission from the vitriolic tirade. I quickly inserted myself into the sliver of silence, stood, and began to testify of the sanctity of the family, its eternal nature and its dependence on Christ-like parental virtue and goodness for long term sustenance and stability.

He allowed a grudging silence when I finished. I thanked them for letting me visit and excused myself. Victoria came to the door with me and followed for a few steps outside. It was very cold, a three-quarter-moon was shining and in the half-light I could see her attempt at a smile. It almost broke my heart.

Soon after, Victoria and the children started attending Church on a regular basis. Her husband became even more abusive. When things grew even more intolerable for Victoria and the children she eventually filed for divorce and of course needed a safe haven, a place of spiritual solace. Fortunately, Ann's folks had a summer cabin not many yards from our home on the lake and they were kind enough to let Victoria's little family stay there until they could sweep away the disarray and let things settle.

Our older children, now all grown, still remember Victoria bringing over goat's milk tinted with food coloring—sometimes pink, sometimes green. And I? I remember her smile—no longer tentative, no longer weighed with sorrow, but as bright and as broad as a cloudless summer day. But every time I recall that smile I'm also reminded of a sweet little boy with pure and absolute faith in Christ's guiding spirit. Because of his him the lost was found and brought back into the circle of our Savior's kind and loving care.

We have kept in contact with Victoria over the years. She is doing marvelously well. She and her two youngest children, in their teens, came to visit us a couple of summers ago. They were bright, polite and a joy to be with. And Victoria? Victoria, still has that marvelous smile that warms and enlivens all who are blessed to be in her presence.

The Lost Hike

It's nice to have a friend along when the going gets a bit thick or threatening. An unflappable, phlegmatic, not-given-to-loud-and-whiny-criticism-friend is better still. That's why I was grateful to have Max along the night I got lost in a thousand acre wood just up the hill from our home. Max stuck by my side and uttered not a discouraging or a critical word despite some very dumb moves on my part. The average human would have had a great many reasons to complain. Of course, Max wasn't average, nor, come to think of it, was he human—Max was my dog!

Max and I weren't total strangers to this acreage densely populated with fir, cedar, hemlock, giant maple and thickets of impenetrable underbrush. We'd hiked through it at least a half-dozen times on our shortcut to Kayak Point. Some of the sections were swamps, many were crisscrossed with old windfalls or trees felled by loggers intent on taking only the giant firs. The smaller stuff that got in the way was felled and pretty much left to rot. In short, it wasn't exactly a stroll through a sylvan glade.

I'd told myself on several occasions that taking a compass would be a smart thing to do. So much for smarts. I rationalized that I could always get my east/west bearings from the sun. That argument was about as valid as a check written by a con-artist who'd served time for forgery. After all, we did live in the Pacific Northwest.

My most compelling rational for not taking along any kind of guidance was that we only had to traverse about five miles of deep woods to arrive at our destination. Of course, here in the tail end of the Twentieth Century all of that is a moot point—virtually all of that rugged forest has now been claimed by asphalt and houses. Ironically, none of the roads interconnect so now there is no shortcut to Kayak at all, unless of course you trespass through yards, scale fences, and fend off ferocious Dobermans and Pit

Bulls. Great fun, that!

But back to 1982. It was a fairly nice day in July—perfect for going to Kayak Point and sitting at a picnic table just a few yards from the beach and working on one of my American Reflections (a daily radio syndicated radio commentary that I did at the time). Of course, Max was ready to go at the hint of any outward movement. One of the reasons that I loved going to Kayak was that in fair weather there were often spectacular sunsets over the waters of Port Susan as the golden orb sank below Camano Island. The sun was pretty much in control of the sky when we started our trek but by the time we arrived at kayak it had lost some of its clout. I got rather caught up in my writing and wasn't paying too much attention to the time or the weather. I suddenly realized that I was cold when an involuntary shiver gave me a little shake. I glanced up. The sight that greeted me wasn't very pleasant. Storm troopers had arrived in solid ranks-and-files of gray and had sent a chill through all that they commanded. The clouds had banished the sun. With a frown of disappointment I glanced at my watch. It was almost seven o' clock. I had missed dinner. Ann would be worried.

We set off through the woods going at a fairly decent pace. I knew the approximate time that it took for this hike so I glanced at my watch to see if I could better our record. As soon as we entered the dense forest I realized that it was indeed very late to be starting. There were no shadows—I felt directionless, but we plunged on. So did time. I glanced at my watch and saw that we were way overdue for reaching the eastern trail. I reasoned that a course adjustment was needed. But which adjustment? Somehow I felt that I needed to veer more to the left, so I veered and plunged but nothing but ever-darkening woods loomed ahead. I was getting tired. Max kept glancing at me as if to ask, "Er, Master do you really know what you're doing?"

I checked my watch again—our time was almost double! Where were we? I saw a thinning in the black. I ran, I tripped, I got up and ran again! It was a road. Hooray…Thank you dear

God! I felt the gravel under my feet and rejoiced. Then I looked down the familiar road. It was familiar all right! It was the same road that we had started from!

I felt the weight of despair close in and I reached down and gave Max a comforting pat. I was the one drawing comfort. Prudence and wisdom left only one choice—walk down Marine Drive until it intersected with Fire Trail road and just follow it home; straight arrow, no deviations, simple. Sure the mileage was longer but it was sure fire. Ah, but then macho pride reared its swollen head. Surely a little dinky patch of woods wasn't going to stop me. Surely a little darkness and an all too typical Northwest drizzle wasn't going to dampen my now keenly honed deep woods navigational senses? Obviously I had veered to the left on my first time through—this time I will veer to the right and all will be well. Right?

Once again we plunged into the forest. Well, I thought it was 'we' until I had gone about fifteen yards or so and realized that Max wasn't by my side. My troops had abandoned me, my follower wanted to be my leader. I called out to Max. I heard slow, reluctant movements coming through the underbrush toward me. I didn't see Max until he actually brushed against my leg. It was very dark indeed. My watch had a phosphorescent dial so I glanced at it again in the vague hope that it would give me a stronger sense of purpose and I could somehow gauge my progress. I knew that the real question was, 'would I make any progress at all?' Amid all this mental nattering I was uttering, 'Atta boys' and 'Good dogs' in the general direction of Max.

We forged on, always veering to the right, or so I imagined. I was very tired and hungry and it seemed that I was stumbling on, in or around something with every step. Even tiny succulents seemed to reach up and grab my boot. I noticed that the ground was getting as mushy as my brain when suddenly I took a step and sank into muck up to my knees. My momentum carried me forward from the waist up while my legs were being sucked into permanent bondage behind the rest of me. I lay helpless and hopeless, my face and hands groveling in slime while my feet were sucked and stuck in the muck. I managed to drag my left hand toward the one eye now congealed shut with primeval slime and looked at the faintly glowing dial. My, how time flies when you're having fun. I had exceeded the normal trek-time by close to thirty minutes. My spirits sank as low as my submerged feet. We were totally, irrevocably lost.

As I struggled to get my feet unstuck and unmucked I muttered to Max. "If you have any ideas I'd be real happy to hear them."

He responded with a throaty growl.

When I finally got my feet unstuck and on top of the ground I suddenly realized that I was in a kneeling position. How foolish I was. If I had just started this whole little adventure in this position and sought wisdom and guidance from God I would have probably been home showered, fed and sleeping between crisp sheets.

I had literally been pummeled, pushed, and crushed before I was pliable enough to fit into the humility mold. I knew that my ignorance had been monumental as I began one of the most heartfelt prayers of my life. I thanked God that Max and I were unharmed. I admitted freely and most earnestly my gross foolishness and vanity. Tears came to my eyes as I recalled the great blessings of a lovely and loving wife and family and the joy and delight of living in one of the most serene and beautiful spots on earth on the shores of Lake Shorecraft. I was caught in a wonderful stream of thanksgiving, when I suddenly realized that Ann would be worried sick—perhaps even rounding up help. I mustered my thoughts and then asked God for specific help.

I got to my feet and looked around. I felt much better, the night somehow didn't seem quite as black, but I still had absolutely no idea which direction to go. I saw no lights to give directions, no inner voice whispered the path, Max didn't grab me by the wrist to pull me homeward. I stood there…waiting for something, but I didn't know what. Suddenly I heard a strange noise that seemingly came from high in the roof of the dark forest. It was coming from the right. It reminded me of the chittering cries that the Douglas squirrel makes during mating season. But this was steady, unceasing, perhaps a little higher in pitch. I had no other choice. I followed the sound.

We followed it for about ten minutes. Not once did it falter—it was like a well conceived machine in its consistency. It was penetrating and unerringly easy to follow. Then it seemed we had reached its source. The chit-chit-chit was directly above us. I looked up, trying to see what it was, then it stopped!

There was no sound, no movement, nothing but silence. I felt abandoned. I shuffled my feet in agitation, as I did I suddenly realized that I wasn't standing on loamy forest floor but on hard-packed earth—a path. No, not just a path, but *the* path. It was the very path that led down the hill to our home on the shores of Lake Shoecraft. I hugged Max and let out a whoop of joy. Tears of thanksgiving easily came. I didn't care. They were still there when I walked in the door and folded Ann in my mud-encrusted arms and asked for her forgiveness.

Heavenly Squeeze

Yesterday (August 9) the temperature clawed its way up to 87 degrees. Down in Marysville's low lands it hovered in the low nineties—very hot for Western Washington. All of that flat-out sun had warmed the lake by at least six degrees and that in turn precipitated at least a 200 degree jump in activity on the lake. It became a hot cauldron of churning props and jet skis. This morning (the morning after) I hoped to beat the heat, both temperature and activity wise, and have quiet communion with the lake. So at 7:30 a.m., while all peace-corrupting craft were tethered tight to their docks, I slipped into the still waters of the lake. A serene peacefulness reigned over Shoecraft. It was heaven.

Swimming southward my eyes slowly swept the flawless sky and I noticed what was left of the waning moon. That halved-orb, bereft of darkness, looked like an ice-encrusted wedge of lemon suspended in the sky. In my mind's eye I could make out the rind, the segmented flesh, all frostily frozen into place. And as I watched, a silver 777 appeared, as if from nowhere, in that cool palette of pale blue and hoary white and sliced across my lemon in the sky. Just then (miraculously I thought) a small, tear-shaped puff of cloud appeared beneath my lemon moon. Had it felt the squeeze? I couldn't help my self, my imagination had consumed my thought's flight and my mouth began to pucker with its tease. I had to swallow. Hmmm, not bad, on a sunny August day—lemon aid from on high.

More Than a Machine

The Speaker's hand automatically found the "on" switch for the microphone while he scanned the bills on the day's calendar. He glanced up from his papers to find me. I nodded an okay. The gavel came down three times.

"The House will come to order. The Clerk will call the roll."

"Adams, Amen, Anderson, Backstrom, Bagnariol. ..." The members of the state House formed automatically on my tongue. My pencil ticked behind the names of those who responded and left untouched those who did not.

Five legislative sessions had etched the names and faces into my mind. Only election years and emergencies brought changes. I was beginning to feel like one of the omnipresent machines that helped oil the legislative process. I scanned the chambers and picked up four legislators who had come on the floor late. I quickly tabulated, then announced the roll. "Mr. Speaker, ninety-four present, five absent or excused."

The Speaker rose, announced the flag bearers' names, and rapped the gavel. Ninety-four chairs sighed as ninety-four legislators stood to honor the flags of country and state. All heads turned as the flags were carried with slow strides down the broad center aisle that separated the political parties. The bearers ascended the stairs and crossed to the back of the large Speaker's podium. The flagpoles chinked into the standards and the guest minister arose in a rustle of black robes to offer the invocation. My mind wandered as the prayer began. "And why shouldn't it?" I rationalized. "I've heard all of the carefully polished phrases and clever sayings I can stand in prayers."

"Except the people repent, this land will be cursed with a sore curse! I pray that the people of this state and you, their legislators, will repent of your sins that this state may overcome its grave and serious problems. I exhort these things in Jesus' name. Amen.'"

A jolt of excitement ran through me. Then I did something I hadn't done in five legislative sessions; I turned from the rostrum and strode to the minister, who was just starting to sit down. He straightened when he saw me approach. I shook his hand firmly.

"That's the best prayer I've heard offered in these chambers. It's nice to meet someone with the honesty and fortitude to say what really needs to be said."

"Well, I appreciate your thanking me. I'm not too sure that my prayer was received with the same enthusiasm by the assembled body."

One glance proved him to be right; several unveiled stares iced the spot where we were standing.

"Well, you really didn't expect to tickle their ears, did you? Anyway, I'd like you to know that I appreciate your honesty."

I started to turn back to the rostrum, but I could see he wanted to talk.

"You know," he continued, "a few months ago I wouldn't have given that prayer, but I have been so fired up by some of the lay members in my own church that it has made me come alive. Frankly," he confided, "the church has become a dead horse. Even though we have many millions of members, the church has become lifeless. The only hope is the lay movement in the church." The minister went on to say how enthusiastic he was about some of the laity in his church and how they were trying to breathe life back into it.

I excused myself to read in a senate bill. It was controversial so I knew the debate would be long. That would give me the time I needed.

When I returned, he continued in hopeful terms about the lay movement in his church. When he paused, I interjected, "You know, I have a feeling you would really be interested in the Mormon Church."

"What makes you think that?" A hint of a frown came over his face.

"Well, the things you're missing in your church—you can find them in The Church of Jesus Christ of Latter-day Saints."

While the floor debate droned on, I told him of my conversion to the Church, gave him a capsule version of the First Vision, and a brief outline of some of the Church programs. I sensed that the floor debate was nearing completion and that my time was limited. Our eyes met. His gaze did not waver and I told him that I knew that God the Father and his Son Jesus Christ appeared to Joseph Smith, that the gospel in its fullness was now on the earth. As I bore my testimony, a warm glow kindled within me, and I knew it was emanating from me, for the minister's eyes were still locked on mine. Without hesitation he reached out and shook my hand firmly.

"I believe what you have told me. I can sense the truth of it. Please send me all the material you can on your church."

When the Speaker looked over to see if I was ready for the final vote, I quickly returned to the roll call machine to set up the bill and its number through a switching procedure. The gong signaling the start of the vote brought a scurry of movement as legislators who were not on the House floor for the final debate rushed back to flip their voting tab to yes or no. All eyes were on the big board as the lighted numbers rolled out to seal the fate of the bill.

"Has everyone voted? Does anyone want to change his or her vote? The Speaker will lock the roll call machine; the clerk will take the roll." I pressed hard on the tabulator button. A triplicate sheet of the results slowly emerged from a thin slot in the machine.

The phrase "just a part of the machinery" came into my mind again as I went through the routine of setting up for the next vote. Just then someone touched my shoulder. The minister was standing beside me.

"I appreciate what you have shared with me. Be sure to send that information," he said softly.

He turned and left the rostrum as the session continued. The warm feeling returned to my chest and expanded to fill my whole body. I had been reminded of the joy of sharing testimony—and hoped I would remember that joy, for some time to come.

Two-Million-Mile Nile-Mosquito Eaters

It was the most mellow of mornings —I felt my heart would melt under the spell of its soft serenity. The sky, the sun, the water, the air—all seemed to be holding their collective breath. Even the sound of things didn't seem to be making their waves. I heard no chain saws, no big rigs, no jet skis, no planes—an absolute miracle. The stillness was so profound that other senses stretched to fill the void, I could feel the earth slip beneath my feet.

I too, held my breath for I knew from experience when filming in a wilderness area that it was a virtual impossibility to lay down a track of pristine-sound free from the pollution of man-made things. I had no idea how much audio junk there was until I tried to capture twenty minutes of clean sound. Even when you're in a so-called wilderness area there seems to be a plane prowling or a dirt bike bellowing somewhere just over the hill.

Had both man and nature paused to honor God and the sacredness of the morning? Not too likely, at least on the human side of the equation. Then almost simultaneously I heard the sharp, loud chatter of a Jake-brake from a dump truck and its 'pop' trailer hauling gravel to the new casino going up near by. Before the Jake-brake chatter died I heard the high squeal of a car burning rubber. Even as a teenager the negative economy of leaving even fifty cents of my hard earned tire-rubber on the road dissuaded me from jack-rabbit starts. To escape the ear-quakes I quickly submerged my self in the lake and in an instant the sounds and cares of the world were gone.

As I swam southward I noticed how much lower the level of the lake was after a month and a half without rain. A dozen starlings and one lone robin were taking advantage of our neighbors' newly exposed sandy shore by wading down its gentle slope until they were about knee high into the placid water. Is the spot where birds' twiggy legs hinge back, not forward like we humans, called a knee? Maybe it's an eenk? Well, whatever it's called, they were bending there with great abandon and dunking and dipping down into the water with wildly flapping wings. Cooling, refreshing, cleansing. The droplets of water flying off their wings were caught by the early sun and transformed into a jumble of dancing jewels. I marveled, and felt a small warm twinge in my chest, a twinge I've felt a hundred times before and somehow I've always thought, or imagined, to be some sympathetic rapport with the animals as they experienced the joy of their existence. Foolish, perhaps, but a foolishness that has brought me much delight and joy.

Just three lots further south the whole front edge of the dock was filled with fledgling barn swallows—downy little pilots all atwitter, excitedly waiting for their chance to take off from the deck of their own aircraft carrier. Their heads looked too large for their bodies and their bodies looked too encumbered with puffs and plumes of down to be aerodynamic. But there they were excitedly taking their turn at this thing called flight. I was reminded that it was only a little over a month ago that these same hatchlings were tremulously sitting on the piers and the canvas boatcovers looking fearful and perhaps even skeptical about this whole flying thing. And their parents, the doyennes of downy aerodynamics, were doing their feathered best to cajole and coax—virtually everything short of pushing their babes off their perches to get them air borne. And now, wow! What a difference a few weeks made. They were swooping, soaring, climbing high then diving to within inches of the lakes surface before recovering to the skim mode. I could almost hear their mothers saying, "Now children be careful and don't get too tired. Remember in just a few more weeks we'll have to travel thousands of miles to our winter home. Conserve your strength and concentrate on catching all of the gnats and mosquitoes you can instead of just playing around. Mark my words, you'll need all the strength and reserve you can get for the long flight south. I don't want to hear a chirp out of you about being too tired or, 'When are we going to get there.'"

But those little down balls were so intent on their aerobatics I doubt they heard even one peep of their parents admonitions.

Alexander Wilson, a respected pioneering ornithologist calculated that a barn swallow might in its ten year life span travel over 2,000,000 miles. I'm impressed, particularly if you consider that they might catch fifty or so West Nile mosquitoes for every mile they soar. How could you not give a cheer when you see these formally attired Hirundo rustica soaring and swooping near your home?

The Chiropractic Chorus

There was a brisk northern breeze blowing this morning, not the norm for an August day break, but welcome all the same for there was a '90 degrees and rising' forecast.

When I got down to the dock I could hear, feel and see the scampy wind rushing headlong from the water into the defensive line of trees along the shore. The leaves were applauding the breeze's bold end runs and I imagined myself in one of the best seats in some gigantic bowl game. Even the usually sedate alder leaves were flashing their silvery undersides—a seldom seen show of alder ego, I thought. The Douglas firs, the cedar and the hemlocks, the heavyweights, the line and the line-backers, were bending, twisting, bowing, leaning, then springing back after the gutsy gust's attempted pass. Then the spectators, the lake and I, did the wave for a supportive show of gleeful appreciation.

I imagined the trees woody spines being stretched in some kind of chiropractic chorus—limber lumber in the making. The madrona (strawberry in Spanish because of its bright red berries) was doing its yearly skin shedding, the scrolls of rich coppery bark hanging from the larger branches and the trunk were being unfurled by the ruder blasts of wind only to spring back when the winds subsided, as though protecting some sacred script inscribed on its smooth inner skin. Both Ann and I have been charmed by the madrona, perhaps because of the evergreen leaves and the glossy browns of its bark seems to remind us of warmer climates and balmy shores. The madrona also holds special meaning to some coastal American Tribes in relation to their commonly held belief in the great flood. After the torrents ceased it was a madrona tree on the top of Mount Newton that they were able to tie and anchor their canoe to. Even now, the Saanich people do not burn madrona in their stoves or fires because of the sacred roll it played in giving a safe, strong moorage in the midst of the great flood.

As I swam northward against the wind the waves slap-danced on my head and sprayed behind me, giving, I thought, the illusion of speed. I almost laughed out loud at the idea of me showing signs of swiftness, but still that faux impression pleased the Walter Mitty in me and I let it entertain me for a dozen yards or so. I marveled that all of nature seemed to be in joyous commotion. What fun.

...Another morning and yet another testament that there is joy to be found in virtually every moment and every place if we but take the time to search and observe.

Fall Unraveling

The first school buses of autumn send shivers through me. It's true. Those yellow-carriers-of-children to some endless dolor of desks and chalky dust evoke in me inner prickles of impending loss. Once the diesel-belching yellow dragons start sniffing out the summer-bleached children I know that all that's halcyon and warm will soon be shorn and shrunk.

Long and leisurely swims in the lake will end and the curtains of night will draw ever tighter around the waning windows of winter light. Everything, everything will be foreshortened.

The constraints of ever encroaching dark will make the weight of time seem heavier still. We mortals, already foreigners to time, will count and pray for the day when light will start to spread her wings with ever broader, bolder bands of gold and blue and warmth. Such are the thoughts that impending winter evokes in me here in the Pacific Northwest.

All of those feelings were static-charged and loosely stuffed and jumbled in my mind as I walked our youngest child, Jaime, to the end of our drive to catch her bus on the first day of the school year.

I have always felt that children are especially keen when it comes to reading emotions and thoughts. I could pretend and act all I wanted but I had no doubt that Jaime was not immune to my fall forebodings. She was feeling the same as I about climbing onto that malformed monster that carried little children away from hearth and home. But come it did, the door opened and hissed in true dragon fashion as I lifted Jaime onto the first step of the bus. The driver did her best to smile invitingly at her newest conscript. It didn't work. Jaime turned to me with panic, lunged back into my arms and dug her small fingers into my sweater. I spoke consolingly, I assured her that a fun filled day awaited her. Hypocrite! The driver gave broad nods of affirmation, each nod punctuated with a telling look at her watch. Jaime wasn't buying, then the driver dug into her, surely well practiced, bag of tricks and pulled out a treat. "Ah, see what I have for the children on the bus this morning —your choice of one of these candies."

The treats turned the tide of impending tears but I could tell that a current of apprehension still lingered as I placed her on the steps inside the door. Nevertheless, Jaime turned, put one small foot on the next step up and reached for the lure. The driver's face flashed a look of triumph—the captive was hers! She reefed on the door handle and it swung shut. I heard no sobs —all would be well. The dragon hissed once again and off it rolled down the autumn hued road. It wasn't until the bus started moving that I noticed the tug. My clinging child had taken part of my sweater with her onto the bus. The dragon's closing mouth had ensnared Ann's lovingly knit sweater on one of its bolt like teeth and now both my last-born and my last knit sweater were disappearing down the road. I don't know if knitters have any terminology for the reverse of knit one, pearl two, but whatever it might be it was happening rapidly right there on my very own torso. My sweater was disappearing from the bottom up. I waved my arms frantically hoping the driver would see me in her mirror. She did. Through the bus window I saw her sketch of a wave—her thumb and forefinger had formed a circle of success. The driver's foot, now heavy with conquest, shoved the pedal to the metal. Simultaneously the bus lurched forward and belched a beluga size balloon of sickly-gray exhaust. It hung there in the still autumnal air in the shape of a giant exclamation mark—an odious testament of triumph over tenderhearted fathers, family and hand knit sweaters.

It was with heavy heart and a lightened sweater that I turned and walked down the drive. Would Ann believe my more than bizarre story? Should I take the sweater off and bury it in the garbage can? Perhaps Ann wouldn't miss it, then perhaps she would.

I opted for the truth, strange as it was. Ann listened, suppressed a smile, then gave the hopeful promise that she could mend and re-knit.

Unravelings come into every life. And not surprisingly they come more frequently as the weight of each succeeding year gets heaped unrelentingly on the scale of time. One can only hope and pray that there are loving and willing menders and re knitters standing by when you encounter the yellow dragons of life. Of course the best assurance of that happening is if you can look in a mirror every day and see a loving and willing mender and knitter reflected there.

The Never-Ending Circle

It began (at least for me) when Ann, my wife and mother of our seven children, read a rather amazing true story[3] for our family home evening. As the story unfolded I was touched by the profound effect a simple act of service had wrought on one man's life. However, as Ann was concluding the story, I began to envision a circle that had begun, but was not yet completed. As the circle began scribing itself more firmly in my mind, the more excited I got, for I envisioned the circle always growing —encompassing more and more people as it grew. The more I thought about this "circle of service" the more I wanted to become a part of it.

The New Era magazine story that inspired my "circle" was told by Lindsay Gunnel, a girl in her teens who had been given an assignment in seminary class to give a brief devotional talk on service. Lindsay sought out her Grandmother May for ideas for her talk. Her Grandmother immediately responded, "I think I have just the story for you." Lindsay's Grandma then related an incident that occurred while she and her children were living in Fort Carson, Colorado while her husband, Lindsay's Grandfather, was serving as an Air Force pilot in Viet Nam. A friend of May's had organized a service project of reading to wounded servicemen in the Fort Carson hospital, and one day she asked May if she would mind baking some birthday cakes for some of the men. May, despite her busy schedule and large family, said that she would. The next day May's friend called and asked if she could bake a cake that morning. May said "Yes", then proceeded to make a delicious chocolate cake from scratch, piled high with swirls of rich, creamy frosting.

Just a few hours after her friend had picked up the cake May's phone rang.

---

3 *Nov. 1996 "The New Era" p. 8*

"I thought you'd be interested in what happened with your cake," May's friend said. "I took it to a 36 year-old sergeant, a veteran of many years in the Army, who was recovering from wounds. He looked like a typical, tough drill sergeant without a kind word in his vocabulary. When I took the cake into his room and wished him a Happy Birthday, he had a stunned expression on his face, then tears started rolling down his cheeks. The sergeant said that this was the first birthday cake he had ever had. Nobody had ever cared enough in his entire life to bake him a cake."

The next morning as Lindsay related the remarkable story to her seminary class, she noticed that her teacher had an incredulous look on his face. Lindsay was concerned that perhaps her story wasn't what her teacher had hoped for. When she concluded her talk, her teacher asked "Lindsay, what is your Grandmother's name?"

Lindsay felt that her story was so unbelievable that her teacher was going to check with her Grandmother to verify it. But her concern was quickly allayed when her teacher said, "Lindsay, I know the sergeant that your Grandmother baked a cake for. He's told me the story about the cake. He had always wished that he had known who had baked it so he could thank her."

Then Lindsay's teacher looked right at her and said, "Lindsay, that cake wasn't just a birthday cake. It was the beginning of a whole new life for the sergeant. Class," he continued, "I want you to know that Lindsay's Grandma's act of service literally changed that sergeant's life. Before he was wounded, he was pretty mean. Every other word out of his mouth was a swear word. After he received that cake in the hospital in Colorado, he decided to change. He told me he was going to try harder to be a better person, and that's just what he did."

Well, the foregoing is an abbreviated version of the story that set my circle in motion, so to speak. Often, timing is everything, and since I had an assignment to speak in the Marysville 1st Ward the following Sunday (a mere six days away) I thought that retelling Lindsay's story, with a small addition, would be the perfect opportunity to start expanding the "circle of service."

I enjoy making bread, not cakes, so I thought that I would bake a loaf of bread to take with me to Sacrament meeting and give it away, but only after I had told Lindsay's story.

On Saturday I took out some of my best wheat, a high-protein, rich-flavored variety grown in Montana. (I had actually read a letter from the farmer who raised it near the little town of Saco, and talked to the man who cleaned and bagged the wheat.) In short, the wheat really meant something to me. I put the wheat berries into my Country Living Grain mill, a mill that I actually manufacture myself, then I climbed on the exercycle that I have connected to the mill and ground the flour while I read the scriptures. (Could it be the bread would rise higher if I read scriptures while I ground the wheat?) I wanted to be body and soul into this loaf of bread! Everything was ready for the Sabbath.

For freshness' sake I got up early Sunday morning and kneaded all the ingredients, let it rise, then shaped and braided it into a long loaf. I put ice cubes in the oven to give the bread a crisper crust. My special loaf was still hot and wafting marvelous aromas as I walked into the chapel. Three different people indicated that they would like to buy the bread. One sister offered two dollars for it, and when I said it wasn't for sale, she pulled her husband over by the lapel and said, "Honey, give him three."

I related Lindsay's story during my talk, then expressed my feeling that the circle of service and miracles would encompass someone in the congregation, and I asked for everyone to prayerfully consider who they might touch if they gave the loaf of bread to them.

Chad Collins, a fifteen year-old sitting in the front row, raised his hand and said that he would take the bread. After the meeting Chad approached me and said, "Brother Jenkins, I'm not sure who I'm going to give this to, but I think I'll be inspired to know."

I put my hand on his shoulder and said that I was sure that the Lord would inspire him. I asked him to let me know how it turned out. I didn't have long to wait.

A week later Ann and I invited a neighbor (Laurie Bornkamp) to a fireside at church. As we started to leave the chapel after the meeting, a woman stepped in front of me and stated with intensity, "Jack, I've got to talk to you!"

My initial impression was that she was upset with me.

"I got your loaf of bread." she continued.

By then I noticed tears on her cheeks and I thought that receiving the bread had offended her. Perhaps she thought that receiving the bread was sort of a public announcement that something in her life had to be put aright.

My first impression, as is often the case, was not entirely correct. This interesting series of events had taken place:

She (Sister Coy) on the way home from Sacrament meeting said to her husband, "Greg, what would you have done with the bread if Brother Jenkins had given it to us?"

"Frankly, I was thinking of eating it," he smiled, then continued, "What would you do with the loaf it you had it?:

"Well, you remember the big argument over religion I had with our neighbor?"

Greg remembered well.

His wife continued, "We haven't spoken for two years, and I heard from one of her children that she is sick. Well, I thought it would have been nice to take the loaf of bread and some hot soup over to her." Then with visible relief she concluded, "But since we don't have the bread I guess I don't have to worry about it."

Chad, in the meantime, had taken the loaf of bread home and started to pray about who he should give it to. Names came to mind, but none of them stood out. He talked to his parents and asked them for suggestions. Still he felt he hadn't found the person the Lord wanted him to give the bread to. His mother left for choir practice and while she was gone, Chad prayed again. This time Chad knew he had the right person. So, a little after 8 p.m. Chad went to the Coy's, knocked on the door and when Sister Coy opened it, the first thing she saw was the loaf of bread. The first thing she heard was Chad announcing that the bread was meant for her. The first thing she felt? Irritation! She now had to follow through with her good intentions. Her words must become action. Then the spirit distilled on her mind and she graciously accepted the bread, thanked Chad, then immediately went to the kitchen and found a can of her best chunky soup and heated it up. With soup and bread in hand she went to her neighbor's door and knocked, perhaps not very loudly the first time. After garnering more courage, she knocked more boldly and the door was opened by her neighbor's husband. He saw the tears on Sister Coy's cheeks and invited her in. He put his hand on her shoulder and said, "I'm sure my wife would like to see you."

Bread proffered, she apologized to her neighbor and said in effect that even though they had their differences she felt they could share their strengths. The neighbor tearfully accepted the bread, said that she had wanted to apologize many times for her actions, but couldn't quite bring herself to do it. The once not-so-neighborly neighbors tearfully embraced and the spirit of contrition and humility, the Spirit of Christ, began nourishing and healing.

The circle continued to grow. The next Sunday during Relief Society there was a pause in the proceedings, and Sister Coy felt compelled to relate her experience and bear testimony of the power of Christ. She stood and did just that. Even though she had planned to leave immediately after she spoke, she felt prompted to sit down and wait. In a few moments a woman who had been investigating the Church for some time (Kim) rose to her feet and with an emotion-filled voice, said that while Sister Coy was bearing her testimony, the Spirit had borne witness to her of the truthfulness of the Church and that she wanted to be baptized. Several weeks later she entered into the waters of baptism.

I recounted the "Never Ending Circle" bread story while on assignment in the Camano Ward. After I concluded my talk I wondered, as always, who would pick up the loaf or ask for it. Kirk Wilson, sitting next to me on the stand, mentioned several times that it would be good for his son to give the bread to the irate father of a girl that he had recently baptized. The spirit indicated otherwise. It was then that I noticed Sister Donna Marley conversing with some friends near the front of the chapel. I scanned the rest of the chapel again but my attention was drawn once more to Donna Marley. I stood, took the loaf off the lectern and walked down to her. As I approached her I held the loaf up and said, " I believe this bread is yours."

Tears sprang to her eyes as she confessed, "I had prayed all through the closing hymn that you would give me the bread, but I didn't want to ask for it in case the Lord had someone else in mind. I was only going to take it if you felt inspired to give it to me. I wanted the bread to be from the Lord." I assured her that it was.

Some months later I asked Donna to fill in her segment of the circle. She did:

She admitted that while I was telling the story of the never ending circle during sacrament meeting that she was having mixed feelings. She had a friend that she had wanted to share her testimony with but was having difficulty collecting the courage and creating the right opportunity to do so. Yes, she had mentioned the Gospel to her friend before but there hadn't been a blossoming into spirit-felt, heart-touching conversation. Sister Marley longed for that. Now, the Lord had sanctioned her desire by putting the bread specifically into her hands when it could have gone to one of the other two hundred or so people assembled in the chapel. Several weeks later I talked to Donna: the bread had opened yet another door and provoked yet more tenderness and understanding. What a wonderful sense of fulfillment to know that the bread that you knead and bake can rise beyond its physical properties (the loaf) to help inspire others to accept the Bread of Life.

Heaven Scent

It was a couple of weeks before Christmas and I was roaming through the local home and garden store looking for some inspiration. I found myself in the garden department, which I often do, but found little besides bags of moss killer. It was pretty barren—spring was just a glimmer in the purchasing agent's eye, not a reality on the shelves. Empty of heart and hand I turned to leave through the nearest checkout stand and exit, which happened to be just a few yards from me, and as I turned to my left there was a soldierly row of perfectly quaffed miniature Christmas trees, full, dark green.

I wasn't tempted to take one home because we had tried, and failed with a potted, live Christmas tree. So I turned to leave, but, as I did I ran my fingers along one of its boughs in appreciation of its visual beauty and perfect symmetry. Then something as vibrant as a young kitten leaped back at me from the length of my arm and out stretched hand. The rosemary aroma assailed me. I succumbed and breathed as deeply as I could. I withdrew my hand and brought my now waxy feeling fingers to my nose. It was stronger still.

Rubbing my fingers briskly together the friction kindled the rosemary scent to an even greater degree of pungency. The heat fired a bond that was lasting...not in minutes, nor in hours, but years. I bought the rosemary tree, carried it home and put it in a prominent place where I could reach out and rub the needle like leaves of the rosemary. I later transplanted the shrub, tended, watered it and it prospered for several years. It seasoned chicken, new baked potatoes, fish and soups. Yes, and every time I passed it in the yard, I would stop and rub a leaf between my thumb and forefinger and it would bless me with its aromatic presence for hours to come.

When our house burned down the inferno blistered my

rosemary and many of my fruit trees. My rosemary was terminally withered in the blast as were several of my fruit trees, but for some reason I mourned my 'Rosemary' the most.

The Quiet Congregation

The sun had yet to shown his face, but the sky was clear and Sol's imminent arrival was presaged by the faint back-lighting that casts everything in the fore as darkling silhouettes. As I looked just off our shore I could see small, mobile, silent forms crisp against the pre-dawn white of the lake: feathered congregates in front of the dock meeting and milling in quiet communion. I wondered if they could be ring-necks.

I hoped so, for just two weeks prior I had discovered my first ring neck ducks. I suspect they had visited the lake many times before. I probably just hadn't observed closely enough to see the white band near the tip of their bills plus the white ring at the base where bill and feathers met. Their bills also were flatter, more shovel like than the sharper more pointy bills of the fish ducks such as the Mergansers. Since aquatic plants and roots were the ring neck's mainstay you could see how useful their little front-loader shovels could be.

Drama in the Smallest Places

It was a brilliantly sunny day—rare for a Northwest February. When I arrived home it was about four p.m. The sun was casting its late afternoon gold on the far side of the lake and a fair breeze was conducting a chorus of watery lips. I listened to make out the words and as I breathed in the pre-dusk beauty the lake sang out "Come, join me. You and your kayak can be part of the harmony, your paddles can be percussion, hurry, come join me."

If I could out race the shadows to the eastern shore I too could be brushed with warmth and gold before the earth turned her other cheek. But alas, there were interruptions and by the time I made it into the kayak the sun's rays were bent and faded.

But dusk would do, the perspective would become softer still. As I approached the southern cove I heard the Whup, Whup, Whup of giant wings catching great gulps of air. I looked up and saw a Blue Heron launch himself from the top of a towering fir. I paused and watched in awe-filled silence as the heron compressed the darkling mist beneath his wings and disappeared into the gathering dusk. When I could see no more I dipped the paddles into the now still waters and continued round Shullenberg's island. I peered intently down into the dusky water trying to avoid the submerged boulders resting on the northern shoal of the island.

My little windancer already bore two long gouges on the hull left by my careless traversing of these shoals. Looks aren't everything, true, but deep gouges are unseemly scars that could easily lead to leaks. Suddenly another sound broke from above, this one a quicker beat than the great and ponderous heron wings. The stark white head was like a beacon against the blackened sky. He too had been in a fir tree and followed the same Nor'east route as the Great Blue, but with a much higher trajectory.. I tracked the telltale white as far as dusk and aging eyes would allow. I had witnessed a wondrous double treat. I was thankful I had answered the siren song of the lake. I savored the moment in silent thanksgiving, trying not to move a muscle, but the kayak's momentum was cutting a silent and soft edged V in the placid waters.

Gazing at the mirrored lake I suddenly realized that the water was covered with hundreds of tiny feathers, some curled in downy 'O's', buoyantly drifting in an ever growing circle. In an instant the story replayed in my mind. The eagle had landed… and dined. A small duck, a coot to be exact, had been nature's sacrificial offering, it's soft curled down a mute reminder of the cycle of life.

Drama abounds in the smallest of places.

The Bellweathers of Spring

It was a little after one in the afternoon in late April. I was homeward bound from church in my aging cranberry pickup, which I had driven because of an early morning leadership meeting, effectively precluding Ann and me from driving together. Heading west on 172nd Street I passed the bland bunching of cracker boxes we call our High School and driving a little under 25 m.p.h. in deference to the school speed zone I slowed even more, when suddenly some meteorological choreographer called a halt to the eternal chorus-line of clouds that had been parading at close ranks across our sky for the last month.

A brilliant burst of sunshine was now flooding the school and an adjacent dairy farm that had been cow-less for over a decade. I was so bemused by all of the warmth and light that I wanted to park and bask in the glory of it all, besides I could see in the distance the shadows of heavy clouds lurking just beyond the next rise in the road. All in all, the light blazed moment was a rare and welcome respite from the previous weeks of drizzle, drip, and dipping degrees.

So bathed in sumptuous sunshine I was in no hurry to reach a destination besmirched by gray. I glanced into my rear view mirror, saw no following car, slowed even more, then rolled down the window to let in the bouquet of sun kissed air. I was breathing in a deep drought of spring elixir when suddenly a din of great dimension exploded through the window.

The sound was akin to a herd of buffalo racing through a field of wet balloons. A cacophonous chorus of liquidy croaks splattered my ear drums and bounced around the cab of my truck. The sun had worked its warm wonder and provoked a road side bog of frogs into a phonic frenzy. I laughed out loud at the surprise and joy of it.

It was no small laugh; it came from deep down, I swear every cell in my body had joined in—every corner of my mind was alight with delight.

Ten minutes later as I turned down our drive the clouds were having their way once again, but I was still smiling and random chuckles were still escaping from my lips.

Bless the frogs. Bless the sun. And bless me that I may always find joy in small and simple things of life...which probably aren't all that small and simple at all —especially to the frogs, the bell-wethers of spring to come.

The Secret Spy

The summer of 2004 has been warm and dry. Often the highs were in the upper eighties and occasionally nudged into the nineties. A little over a week ago some serious, not cirrus, clouds rolled in tugging along a whole train of rain with them. As of this morning the dump was still in progress and the caboose still wasn't on the horizon. The lake temperature had reached as high as seventy-seven by the first of August, but now with eight or nine drizzled days and nights working their will the chill has shoved the temperature down into the sixties—sixty-nine to be exact.

I had almost forgotten the joys of sunless, rain spiked swims; swims that if they last too long, bring whispers of hypothermia. So it was a wonderful moment yesterday morning about seven o'clock that let me revisit a little quirk of hydro-physics that always brings a sense of awe and delight. As I was swimming toward the south end of the lake the morning drizzle got a little heavy handed and large drops began pelting the lake. What fun it is to be up close and personal when big drops 'kerplunk' just inches from your eyes. Suddenly as far as you can see liquid cones are rising like Phoenix from the surface of the lake. And then miracle of miracles on top of each crystal cone rests a perfect pearl of water. Is that resurrected liquid pearl the same drop that just dropped from the heavens a nanosecond before? I may never know. But since all things will be resurrected perhaps I'm seeing a shadow of things to come.

And there was more: The heaviest drops left yet another brief but beautiful legacy behind. Each transformed drop affixed a final vestige of its former self to the lake's surface. Fairy-wing-thin walls of water formed a bubble that capped each spot where the hydro-sculptures once had been. These bubbles too were short lived but if the wind didn't rise above a whisper and the bombarding rain was errant with its aim the life of the fragile spheres were extended to miraculous minutes —ages compared to the life of the cone and pearls that preceded them.

As I swam my senses were filled with natures' effervescent celebration. How blessed I am to be able to swim the sun, but also swim the rain.

I swam as far as Massart's cove then turned and started home, as I neared our dock I glanced up and there was a small plain Jane duck not more than five yards in front of me looking me right in the eye. I had noticed her before, or at least one of her ilk, for several years, never in a pair or a flock, but always alone. She seemed secretive or maybe a ducks' version of shy. This small recluse seemed to be a year round resident and I've noticed that in the winter when the very social coots (mud hens) come flocking in that my shy, mousey little friend will hang around with them, generally the periphery, but she doesn't seem to mind the company at all. Even when the pushy mergansers arrive with their fish pillaging armadas she still hangs around. To me she has been a mystery woman. I have leafed through my bird books but never felt I had a perfect match, besides I had never been able to get a really good look at her, even with my binoculars. It seemed she had some sixth sense: every time I focused my binoculars on her she would slip under the water. And slip is a good word, for she didn't seem to expend any energy when she dove. For example the mud hens often seem to elevate off the lake, catch air as a snow boarder might say, and plunge under with gusto. But not my secretive little sister, she seems to be able to sink right straight down like a submarine taking on ballast —nary a ripple in sight. In fact on a couple of occasions I could have sworn that her little black eyes still protruded, periscope like, above the surface still checking the sea-scape for eminent danger. I suspected I was delusional about the periscope eyes, but still it intrigued me. But this morning she was so close I could see details unseen before. I tried to hold her image in my mind. I rushed in from the lake, rinsed off and did a brisk towel down, then went immediately to the downstairs book shelf and pulled out the North American Bird

Book (a gift from Joel) published in England. The color plates are gorgeous, the details crisp and clear. Suddenly there she was, my homely little plain Jane in muted browns and gray. I read the text, then read it again and laughed out loud:" pp 17 "..when threatened, it can sink below the surface of the water with only its head showing, like a submarine with the periscope up."

Vindicated! I had not been delusional, Now, my little secret spy had a name—the Pied Billed Grebe. Her name was about as homely as she was, but all in all a good fit. Now when I swim I can greet her, "Hello Grebe." Perhaps she will recognize her name and hang out with me for moment or two before she practices her periscope routine: Yet another joy to add to my list.

Postscript:

Grebe again.

When I went to the lake this morning, October ninth, I heard great sounds of splashing. I thought, perhaps somebody in a paddle boat was coming into shore. What I saw instead were two ducks chasing, frolicking? I looked again—two grebes! Then as I strained to see, in unison and in true grebe-like fashion,they sank stealth-like below the darkened surface. She had a friend. Terrific and wow! I've never seen a baby grebe before...another joy to anticipate.

The Moon and Me

I slipped into the lake at 6:20 this morning. The sky was clear with thin clouds on the eastern horizon. The sun probably wouldn't make it over the tips of the firs and cedar until about 7:00. I hate seeing the dark getting a bigger grip as each day passes but, now that the earth is into her autumnal turning the sun is forced into evermore tardy arrivals and early retirements. The mercury too mourns the loss of the sun and sinks into depression. I checked the thermometer under Dick's dock and found the mercury had sunk to sixty-six degrees—a far cry from the high seventies four weeks ago. I wondered how long the sixties could hold on. I wondered how long I could hold on swimming when the sixties say sayonara and the fifties show their pinched and chilly faces? Time will tell. Time, this unreal reality that eventually will reveal all.

I started swimming south and scanning the lake for any other early morning travelers and through the rising mist I saw Miss Grebe stealthily fading in and out of the foggy fingers rising from the lake. Then in an instant she was gone. Like Red October she had sunk into the depths. About five minutes later she suddenly appeared about twenty yards in front of me. I said, "Good morning Miss Grebe." I pronounced the 'e' on the end of Grebe. Just plain Greb (Webster's preference) sounds too abrupt, too cold. She seemed to listen and swam closer. I continued to talk to her in soft tones. She mutely swam and intently looked and listened for three or four minutes, never stopping her observation as I swam. A little bank of fog rolled between us and when the breeze thinned the mist, Miss Grebe was gone. Tomorrow, perhaps I'll see her again.

By now the sun's rays reached beyond the trees and had begun to ignite the surface of the lake. Suddenly the vapors lost their haughty airs, bowed in submission and snake-like slinked into nothingness. A golden glow bathed the western shore and windows reflected back their burnished treasure. I rolled and swam on my back and while scanning the perfect blue of the morning sky I discovered a frosty smile affixed in the heavens directly above me. There it was, that frozen wedge of lemon that I'd seen before, still waiting to be squeezed. And even though I'd seen that half moon, pale against the competing sun many times before I still felt the hint of a pucker while staring at that lemon slice suspended in eternal space. The half moon in daylight had lost its gold and taken on a hoary white, the outer edge, more solid, formed the icy rind. The segments of lemon were less distinct but my imagination easily filled in the blanks, so once again I could almost taste the lemon-sour and my mouth began to water because the hint of pucker was so strong.

My eyes searched beyond the edge of the slice and there it was, the ever so faint outer rim of the unlit portion of the moon. I was floating in my own private sea gazing heavenward, my ears submerged, muffling earthly sounds to extinction. If there were any lunar voices to be heard space had sucked them into eternal silence. So there we were just the moon and me, both held in place by some celestial string, both snug in our appointed slot in space. The Moon smiled down on me. I smiled back. Then, a surge of unnamed feelings—a warmth spread from my chest outward into my limbs. Suddenly nothing existed in all of space save two bodies, one telestial, one terrestrial. I became transfixed and swore I could feel the moon-tugging, lifting, pulling me up.

What celestial forces kept us both in place, so still, yet hurtling at blinding speed through space? My mind seemed to burst with the enormity of it. I felt myself being drawn toward the orb suspended directly above. The moment passed but the remembrance stayed. I'll reread this story from time to time to revisit, knowing the power will never be the same but a patina of awe will certainly linger.

The Rain Drenched Prayer

It was a sodden and rainy October afternoon, common fare for the Pacific Northwest. Amy Williams, mother of three, already running late, was frantically trying to get her children, one through six, ready to go on a grade school sponsored 'pumpkin run'. Things were not going smoothly: her three year old announced that he'd had an accident—his euphemism for four months of potty training gone awry. Her year old redhead, with a temperament matching both her age and her hair, was lustily objecting to anything and everything. Her six year old, whose class was taking the pumpkin farm outing, was bemoaning the fact that heaven was favoring Noah more than the first graders from Cougar Creek Elementary.

It was at this crucial moment of chaos that the doorbell rang. Feeling the weight of yet another delay looming just beyond the door, Amy, with the sudden heat of a bulb about to burn out, wrenched it open with the words, No, No and No firmly fixed on both her visage and her tongue. The opened door framed two young women, damp but smiling: the sister missionaries. Amy hastily did her best to rearrange her face and her attitude and invited them in.

She apologized for the pandemonium, explained the circumstances, all the while trying to corral her little strawberry blond for a clothes change. The Sisters asked if they could help. "Well no, not really."

"Perhaps you have any neighbors who might be interested in the Gospel?"

"Actually, our next door neighbors are wonderful. We really love them, and he used to play basketball at one of our buildings in Oregon. They might be interested."

With that word of encouragement the Sister Missionaries left and immediately slogged across the boggy lawn toward the neighbor's house. Curious, Amy went to the window to see what degree of success the Sisters might be having. What she saw instead was her six year old, Alyse, kneeling in the middle of the rain drenched lawn praying. Amy admitted that her first thought was rather mundane: Alyse must be praying for the rain to stop so her school activity could be more fun. She soon repented of her shallow conjecture. Alyse, after what seemed like long moments, arose from her knees and came in doors. She was soaked.

Her mother asked, "What were you doing Sweetie?

"Oh Mommy," Alyse replied with pure sincerity, "I was praying to Heavenly Father that the Schultz's would let the Missionaries in and that they would join the Church."

Her mother was moved to tears by the purity of her faith and enfolded Alyse in her arms, "Oh Sweetie, I'm sure Heavenly Father will hear your prayers, but remember," she said, ever the pragmatist, "we will still have to do our part to help the Schultz's learn more about Jesus Christ and his Church."

Alyse solemnly nodded and left.

A few moments later Amy noticed that Alyse was earnestly writing something on a sheet of paper. Alyse looked up and asked, "Mommy, how do you spell, Dear?" Her mother walked over, realized that Alyse was beginning a letter and spelled out, "D.E.A.R." for her.

She then watched as Alyse, in the wonderful, open script of a six-year old, full of faith and nothing doubting, wrote, "Dear Ryan and Sarah, We hope that you will come to Church with us this Sunday, Love, Alyse.

Angel Beam

Ann and I went to Jason and Marli's this afternoon to watch their two little guys so Jason could have some free time for studying and scripting a film for the City of Snohomish. Marli is still working a part-time shift at UPS, a financial necessity, while Jason is struggling to get enough time for school, his emerging film business and do a credible job of watching over Killoran and baby Kelvin while Marli is at work. The heavy hand of life is pressing hard. Life is not an easy balancing act for a young family.

We ordered some Chinese to stave off the pangs of hunger and to help save Jason and Marli's larder from further depletion. After placing the phone order I realized that I didn't have any change to tip the delivery boy, so I took little Ki by the hand and we walked east. Four blocks and seven snarly, yappy little dogs later we arrived at Sam's Sports and Surplus. The only surplus I noticed was sticker shock. I had encountered the woman at the

cash register before—her forte a year ago was certainly not cus-
tomer relations. Time had not softened the granite. As we walked
in the store I could see that her face was still as I remembered, frozen in perpetual annoyance. I began to doubt whether we would
leave with change for the twenty. However, with Chinese waiting
in the wing I mustered up my best smile, held up my limp twenty
and asked if she could possibly change it? The frowning curl of
her lips compressed even more into twin, bloodless lines pointing down—a giant brad poised and ready to pierce my small but
rising balloon of hope. Her eyes narrowed with the displeasure of
opening the till without a sale. I managed to keep a hopeful look
on my face, but I could feel and see a "no" rising in her throat. I
quickly leaned over and picked up Ki and said just loud enough
to catch her multi-jeweled ear, "Ki, look, this nice lady is going to
give us change."

Two-year-old Ki, with his magnificent mop of dark curly
hair and the face and smile of an angel, repeated back with a voice
as innocent and pure as a spring breeze:

"Nice lady."

At the sound of his voice she prized open her squinty eyes
just enough to glance at Ki, then she quickly looked away. But
she wasn't fast enough, an angel beam of light had radiated from
little Ki and somehow penetrated her stony façade. The purity
of a child had touched her wizened soul. She paused and grum-
mumbled something that resembled, "Well, there ah, might, ah,
be enough change in this other drawer."

We made it home just as a kid of Nordic stock drove up with
the Chinese. I asked him how the food was. "Well, ah, I really
don't know because I never eat Chinese there. But then, in a less
than heart felt effort to put a band aid on his public relations gaff
he mumbled, "But I do remember hearing somebody saying that
it wasn't too bad."

Wow, ringing endorsement. Strike one.

"Is the cook Chinese?" I ventured.

"I dunno, but he speaks with a Russian accent."

Woops, strike two: I wasn't too excited about no spices, no
veggies and no endorsement stir fry. But hunger often overrules

common sense, so I held out the tip, smiled then gestured toward little Ki and said, "Consider yourself lucky, if it hadn't been for my grandson you probably wouldn't have gotten a tip at all."

The driver's expression was a perfect reflection of "How weird can this guy get?" He raced to his little Geo, jumped in and left with as much speed as his Geo could muster. He was still shaking his head as he turned at the end of the block.

I smiled at Ki and thanked him for being a good boy and for adding a bit of spice to a meal that held scant promise for epicurean excellence. He smiled back, probably understanding little more than that I was pleased with him. I took the take-out cartons into the kitchen dished out the stir fry and rice onto our plates. We asked a blessing on the food. I was thankful, thankful for wonderful grandchildren, and thankful that we had food to eat, any food at all.

Touched by Humility

I drove my old cranberry pickup down our drive about 7:30 p.m. The weather had cleared and the setting sun was still warming the eastern side of the Lake with its golden rays, and miracle of miracles, all of the speed boats were tethered; there was no roiling of lake or air. I hastily got in my trunks and started swimming to the south end of the lake.

A boy unknown to me was on the end of one of the docks fishing. I circled out around his fishing line so it wouldn't be disturbed. "Have you caught anything?" I inquired of the young fisherman. "No, but I'm humbled just to sit here on the lake and see its beauty. The fish don't even need to bite."

I was choked with emotion: This, from the mouth of a teenager, or anyone's mouth for that matter? Had an angel slipped down from heaven?

I hoped fervently that he would still be there when I returned so I could be touched by more of his goodness. However, the dock was empty on my return and there were no cars in the drive. Pity, for to be in the presence of pure humility is such a rare and precious thing.

Call of the Loon

Nothing that I know of can evoke tingly skin-prickles as surely as the pathos filled cry of a loon, so when I saw a pair of largish ducks flying survey circles around our modest lake my pulse did a little tattoo of anticipation. But the tattoo hushed to a meek muffle when I considered that fish ducks probably have an inborn sense about potential food sources: surely a loon would know that the lake they were considering (my lake) was woefully bereft of fish. I pushed the thought aside, wished for their landing anyway and rushed inside to get my binoculars.

By the time I'd retrieved them I couldn't find the ducks; maybe their fish radar had come up with zip, nada, nothing. Darn. Perhaps they'd winged their way to fishier pastures. I scanned the lake anyway. I visually swept each watery nook and cranny several times before I saw what I'd longed for: The unmistakable, spot-on silhouette of a Loon. Their big velvet-black, princely heads with bills tilted slightly up are the very essence of royal snootyness, and their royal hindmost, bulky as they are, do a great imitation of a submarine on its way under, practically invisible from a distance.

I'm told that a loon's bones are denser than other ducks of their feather, therefore heavier, allowing the loon to submerge faster and deeper while on fishing forays. I hoped it was true because on our lake they were going to need all of their god given skills plus a lot of duck luck to get a belly full during their stay on Shoecraft. I took pleasure in watching them for a few minutes: they didn't dive, not even once.

Just as I thought, their fish sonar probably came up a big negative in the fish department. Maybe they were just grabbing a little respite and not really looking for supper at all. After all heavy bones probably don't make for great aerodynamics, they were probably just tired of keeping that bony ballast air born. What ever the reason for their presence, I welcomed them with warmth and wished them a lengthy stay. It was a wish that bordered on selfishness because what I really longed for was to hear that which only a loon can do.

It was a relatively busy day and of course I couldn't hang around the lake just waiting for a hoped for Loony Tune.

I had some friends, neighbors, who were wrestling with more than a few heavy burdens, I spent some time with them. One of our suppliers just couldn't seem to prioritize a project that was urgent to us but obviously not urgent to him, I spent some time with him. A competitor seemed to take great delight in fabricating fantastic fiction about his grain mill in an effort to cast our tried and true Country Living in a negative light, I didn't spend time with him. Instead we purchased one of his mills, tested it, had others test it and knew that soon the word would be out, despite the huge amount of money they were throwing into magazine ads: his mill just flat out didn't even come close to what they claimed. Several of our children were facing some formidable problems. In short, I had more than enough to be concerned about, all worthy of prayerful consideration.

By then it was dusk and miraculously there were no speed

boats on the lake. The lake called, I came. The winds from north and the winds from south had tendered a truce and in mere minutes the lake's skin had healed to a fine flatness: a forever sheen that begged for a polished pebble to be cast. I searched and found a flint far from polished and slightly more fat than flat, but with hope, I cocked my ageing arm and imagined the fleeting kiss of stone on water trailing forever-dimpled-rings into the fading light. My mind's eye saw the circles grow, touch, then interlock in silent harmony. Eternity encapsulated in a hush.

Ah, but my imagination and reality didn't match. My pebble made two feeble attempts at skipping then sank ignominiously into the depths. Worse yet, the stone's final word at the moment of its watery death held no poetry at all. Its last utterance was an uncouth, rather rude, GLOUUpp !!! I smiled, yet another former skill squished smaller by time and gravity. Betimes Mother Nature seems heavy footed when she's applying the brakes of mortality.

I eased myself into the water's embrace and in an instant I could feel the sundry stresses being tenderly tugged at, watery lips nibbled at the dross of the day, I could feel it drift away.

I rolled on my back and began a slow kick, a fast kick at my age is nothing more than memory gone amuck. The waning moon looked down with her crescent smile. I smiled back and as I did a great flood of gratitude grew with in me. And with that flood my already water washed face became tinged with brine of my own making. The goodness of God, the beauty of His creation, the sure knowledge that Ann, our children and our children's children would be together for all eternity, filled me with a joy and love that I could scarce contain.

I know that God can hear the smallest of voices in the most humble of places, but I suddenly was struck with the thought that I was floating in a giant parabola of sorts, a speaker of terrestrial proportion. Would He think me vain or foolish if I prayed from the center of a 300 acre woofer: better yet, because it was a lake surely a sub-woofer would be the speaker of choice. And the tweeters? Well, the tweeters had to be the lily pads nestled in the darkling coves.

I laughed out loud. God knew well my surplus of vanity and

foolishness. Would he frown or smile at my use of His precious lake as a giant transmitter for my paltry prayers?

I hoped for His smile and swam to the center of the lake. Would the fish be able to hear? It seems precious few still swim our beleaguered little lake. And the turtles, those lovely orange and grey bellied Western Painted Turtles, what of them? I feared they and their habitat had been shredded to extinction by the monster wakes that pound the summer shores of Shoecraft. I hadn't seen a hint of the Western Box Turtle in years. The design on their bottom side is a marvel, it reminds me of a Native American Totem of sorts, or perhaps it's a glyph from a sacred Mayan codex just waiting to be deciphered. But the Axtell's, our neighbors to the south, vowed that they had seen a turtle in Massart's cove.

The very thought brought cheer to my heart. I hoped the turtles were awake and listening. I would pray for them too. The list went on, then I remembered the morning visitors; the loons, were they still on the lake? I hoped so, for as far as I knew they had been silent since their decent to the lake. Had they left without saying goodbye? They too would be on the list.

I floated on my back. My ears were submerged, my arms and hands moved under the surface for silence sake. I spoke in a natural voice and was surprised and a bit embarrassed at how loud it seemed. Way too loud. Was I the magnet in a speaker cone with all of nature the amplifier? I lowered my voice to a whisper, the lake replied with soft acceptance, I felt it hunker closer and enfold every word, each a pearl with a depth and beauty all its own. With the water compacted against my head and ears there was an eerie unearthly resonance that seemed as thick as whipping cream. Surely the languid layering of conjoining sounds were working some hydro magic that would beam all heart felt prayers to the very vaults of heaven?

I swam, I prayed, I floated, I prayed … for close to twenty minutes. On my way back I realized that I was shivering. Both exhausted and exulted I pulled myself upon the dock. The air was colder than the water and I was reminded for the bazillionth time that it doesn't take long for a lake's mid-sixty degrees to pull your bodies core temp into a thermal tail spin. I reached for my towel and started to give my arms a brisk rub down. I could feel the goose bumps greeting the friction with painful pleasure. It was then that I heard it: a melodic mix of hope and haunting pathos: a primal flame parting the mortal dross of present and past. Suddenly, I had new tingles, could loon bumps co exist atop the chill-stirred bumps of another feather? Tingle upon tingle: I knew my prayers had been heard. I had heard God's answer, body and soul!

My Battle with World Famous
Mountain Climber Lou Whittaker

The phone call was a total surprise, from a source never even dreamed of.

The caller identified herself as the regional coordinator of the Mothers of Multiples, a national organization of moms of twins, triplets and course any number of babies beyond that. Bless them a hundred fold, they need all the blessings they can get.

In a very pleasant tone, one well-modulated for soothing fussy babies, or husbands, I thought, she said that she was a faithful listener to my syndicated radio commentaries, American Reflections. My commentaries were broadcast five days a week on three stations in Washington State at the time so I asked which station she listened to. "Oh, KIXI in Seattle," she replied, "And, I really look forward to hearing you every day. I especially enjoy the family vignettes. I can really relate to them." I was pleased.

She continued, "We are holding our Regional Convention in Seattle next month and we would like you to be our keynote speaker." Upon hearing that request I was more than pleased. In fact my ego began to expand and ascend co equally, a precipitous preamble to peril I learned. She paused briefly, then added, "And we have also invited all of our husbands."

"Wow, they must really like me, to invite their husbands. What a powerful draw, a magnet of massive magnitude: Me!"

She paused again, then there a small nervous clearing of throat, " Ah, to be fair I think I should mention that we had originally invited Lou Whittaker to be our speaker...I..I guess you've probably heard of him?"

Heard of him!? Of course I'd heard of him. Lou Whittaker, World famous Mountain Climber: He had ascended virtually all of the most dangerous, breath-takingly-lofty peaks in the world, not to mention conquering Mount Rainier over 200 times. Suddenly Lou Whittaker was my nemesis: I was wishing that I'd never heard of him. My ego was as riddled as a target at a rifle range. I was beyond deflated: I was compost waiting to be buried. How could I ever deliver, ever assume to ascend to the expected heights of the all- too-soon to be assembled mass of males?? I would be trying to traverse a testosterone tinged tight rope. HELP!

I frantically tried to form a gracious, 'Thanks, but no thanks' as a response to her proffered invitation, but cowardice and graciousness are foes from the beginning. Somewhere during my emotional collapse I thought I heard her say that Mr. Whittaker's 'no show' had something to do with a contractual obligation with Nike or some such sponsor. I found no comfort in knowing that while Lou was counting his millions I was sweating bullets. I paused and prayed that graciousness would gain a foothold on the slippery slope I was on. I took a deep breath and responded as best as I could. "Well, it sounds as if I've got my work cut out for me, but I'm happy (I almost choked on 'happy') to accept your invitation to speak."

She allowed a small laugh and responded, "Oh, I'm sure you'll do really well. And, ah.. I'm sure our husbands will really love you."

Well, I knew that 'husband-love' was more than a bit much, but I thanked her and responded with a small fib of my own.

"I'm really looking forward to speaking to your group and I sincerely appreciate and am honored by your invitation."

I spent a fair amount of time praying during the next three weeks. There were no beams of light, no discernible epiphanies. There was only one thing that remained absolutely clear: I was in way over my head. It was just two days before the day. I was exhausted as I walked out on our deck in the early morning sun. I felt the warmth, the peace, the goodness of the sun, the Graciousness of God. It was then that the self-imposed foggy babel of my mind began to fade. It became as evanescent as the morning mist I was gazing at.

Then it came, as softly as a mouse on tiptoe, a very small and quite voice, perfectly calm. But the reality of its meaning was powerful beyond words. "You are not competing with Lou Whittaker, just speak from your heart, about the things you know well: Families"

Of course! I was invited to speak because my commentaries

were centered on the family. The Family, that was it. No heroics, no danger fraught peaks or deep abysses. I slept well that night.

When I went into the convention hall I was surprised to see how many people were assembled. It was packed. There was a sea of Mothers of Multiples and treading water right next to them was a sea of fathers of multiples. A nervous thread started to worry its way into my thoughts. Then I said audibly, but only so I could hear, "Remember, Families, that's what it's all about."

I had a host of stories about families tucked into my mind and in my briefcase. They were my shield. I clutched them tightly, there was comfort there. There was strength.

I spoke for about forty five minutes. The stories came easily. I felt a rapport grow stronger with each story. Soon there were smiles and even guffaws. I even saw tears wiped away, by both wives and husbands. At the conclusion I thanked them for the opportunity of spending some time with such a wonderful group of people. I expressed the deep and abiding joy I felt to be able to share intimate thoughts about a subject so infinitely good and eternal. The Family. And I meant it with all of my heart.

They arose, the sea of smiling husbands and wives, and applauded, and applauded. I was humbled and filled with gratitude.

A week later I received a gracious thank you note that said in part: We feel it is Providential that Lou Whittaker couldn't come. You gave us exactly what we needed and wanted to hear.